YOU WERE ASKING . . .

YOU WERE ASKING . . .

Questions and Answers about
the Christian Life

DENIS G. CLARK

VICTORY PRESS

EASTBOURNE

ISBN 0 85476 184 5

Printed in Great Britain for
VICTORY PRESS (Evangelical Publishers Ltd)
Lottbridge Drove, Eastbourne, Sussex, BN23 6NT
by Richard Clay (The Chaucer Press) Ltd
Bungay, Suffolk

CONTENTS

"CHRISTIAN" SUPERSTITIOUS TRADITIONS

Q. *Tell me, why do we stand up in church to sing hymns and close our eyes when we pray?*

A. I suppose the first is just an English church custom, while the second is general practice. Neither is commanded in Scripture. In some continental countries, and in most state churches, they sit down when they sing hymns. For my part, I close my eyes when praying so that there is a minimum of distraction from my sight sense, which is only too ready to register things that hinder my attention while praying.

Q. *Isn't it a sin not to close your eyes when praying? I was taught so!*

A. Not at all! Whoever taught you that was following superstitious tradition, not truth; and we are overloaded with superstition in Christianity. We need to get rid of it, all of it—and quickly! Would you think that Peter bowed his head and closed his eyes when he was sinking after that short miraculous walk on the water? He must have had his eyes very much open as he shouted to Jesus, "Lord, save me!" Possibly your teacher was trying to threaten you to behave during prayers, and bound you with superstition unwittingly.

Q. *That sounds right! But aren't some superstitions all right in the Church?*

A. No, definitely not! On this point, among others, Christianity differs from all other religions. The others are filled with superstitious practices, forms and meaningless behaviour. Christians are concerned with spiritual reality alone. People in eastern lands are rejecting their idolatrous religions when they learn that the old practices they so fearfully obeyed mean nothing. This is a wonderful revolution. Similarly, as knowledge increases in the west, many are discovering that most of their forms and ceremonies in Christendom cut no ice, but they are making the fatal mistake of rejecting the living God along with these meaningless practices. Who can blame people for rejecting mere forms, vain repetitions and human traditions which God has never commanded? It is time we declared war on it all and faced up to the New Testament's amazingly wonderful spiritual reality. We should quit living in the Old Testament, with its shadows of the real thing which came alive through Christ.

Q. *Carry on! This rings a bell with me. What is your opinion of the Prayer Book?*

A. It contains some remarkable material, though I prefer the Book of Psalms. But let us get to the real issue by considering what Jesus said to a certain Samaritan woman. She wanted to argue about the location of worship. Jesus swept this detail aside and focused her thinking on a totally new concept by saying, "Neither in this mountain, nor yet at Jerusalem . . . They that worship Him must worship Him in spirit and in truth" (John 4. 21, 24). This statement brought new light to the subject—that worship is no longer connected with places or things, however "sacred", but with God's own Holy Spirit. Mere forms had to give way to the preparation of the life and heart. What do we conclude? That any form of worship without adequate heart preparation and the presence of the Holy Spirit is only a powerless rigmarole. Any words directed to God, with or without the Prayer Book, are vain utterances, unless directed by the Holy Spirit.

Q. *Shouldn't we repeat the Lord's Prayer, then?*

A. If it is just for the sake of tradition, or because it is "the thing we always do here", the answer is, No! In that way it becomes vain repetition, which Jesus commanded us to avoid. When I was a boy at school, the daily repetition of it at morning prayers by lads who had no intention of following its precepts so sickened me that I decided never to use the Lord's Prayer again. I felt it was doing more harm than good. But years later God took me into the very sacred depths of that prayer in such a way that I experienced a breaking of heart and cleansing from sin that was unique in my experience. Now, whenever the Holy Spirit leads me to utter the Lord's Prayer, the words are charged with tremendous force, and are full of inspiration and challenge.

Q. *How on earth did that happen? It needs to happen to me!*

A. I will give you just one example: I only got as far as the opening phrase—"Our Father"—when the Holy Spirit directed me to Malachi 1. 6–11. By the time I got through that, He had sorted out all kinds of priorities in my life, so that I began to honour God as Father, and then I understood why such anger arose in Jesus' heart that He drove out of the temple those who bought and sold the animals for sacrifice. I saw that I had to put God first if I was to call Him Father, and not make merchandise of spiritual things by bringing Him the "left-overs" of my life. I was not to use up my day with lesser things and then offer Him what was left over when I was tired out. Nor was I to live the best part of my life for money-making and offer Him the dregs when I retired from business. In addition, He showed me that it was "*our* Father" and not just "*my* Father". This changed my attitude to all true Christians and broke up the worthless denominational attitude that I had.

Q. *I see. I'll go through that prayer, phrase by phrase, too. What was the greatest thing you got out of the Lord's Prayer at that time?*

A. I suppose the biggest discovery I made was with the words, "Give us day by day our daily bread." Most Christians whom I questioned seemed to think that it was an "insurance clause" against going hungry. One might expect such an attitude in western civilization, but it would break down hopelessly in a concentration camp, for instance. The superstition would disappear quickly under such circumstances. But I found reality in that part of the prayer when I read on into verses 5 to 13 of Luke 11 and saw that the daily bread is not the kind we take between our teeth, but the very real power of the Holy Spirit which makes one an effective witness, even when starving in a concentration camp! Many a Christian in such circumstances has provided "living bread" for his fellow-prisoners, and even for his captors! What victory! How true is the prophecy that in these last days there would be a form of godliness which would deny the power thereof! But thanks be to God for the burning testimony of those who have endured prison for Christ's sake, being faithful to death through the power of the Holy Spirit. What a rebuke to our comfortable brand of Christianity!

Q. *But surely it is all right to recite certain prayers.*
A. Never as mere repetition! Our God is not made of

stone, and we should not treat Him as if He were. He is alive and a Person! He demands worship in spirit and truth.

Q. *What, then, about impromptu prayers that go unanswered?*

A. Exactly! If God is real, so are His promises. God has laws for the answer of prayer, and I would say that this is why Jonah had the sense not to try to pray for deliverance while he was wilfully disobeying God. To pray for deliverance, or healing, or anything else, while sailing out of God's will as Jonah was, is sheer humbug and as superstitious as the prayers to idols of the sailors on Jonah's ship! God answers prayer and is ready to reveal His will and power to and through those who will obey Him. Nothing so destroys a person's faith as to keep on praying with no result—and the fault is never God's!

Q. *What about teaching children poetic prayers?*

A. These could be useful if wisely used, but I regret the day I was ever taught that queer concept of God which goes like this: "Gentle Jesus, meek and mild, Look upon a little child; Pity my simplicity," etc. It produced a very sloppy idea of God in my childish mind, and I hated the moment when I had to repeat those words each night. There was the added agony of the word "simplicity", so hard to pronounce, let alone understand! God does not pity simplicity; He requires it! For, "except ye be converted and become as little children, ye shall not enter into the kingdom of heaven". From their earliest days my own children have been taught to pray sensible prayers with faith, and God has responded to them wonderfully. They *know* God is real! I believe parents should teach their

children to *pray*; otherwise they are taking the direct
route to making infidels of them once they start to
question spiritual reality.

Q. *You've shocked all the questions out of me now.
What's next?*

A. Paul was so hot against the way the Galatian believers carried over practices from defunct Jewish
superstitious religion that he wrote to them and asked,
"Are ye so foolish? having begun in the Spirit, are ye
now made perfect by the flesh? Have ye suffered so
many things in vain?" Mind you, he was challenging
them on a very real matter, namely, circumcision,
which was a covenant God made with Abraham. But
along with altars, priests and other Old Testament
things, they wanted to carry it over into New Testament reality, where Christ replaces the Old Testament
shadows and only circumcision of the heart bears any
significance. Paul upbraided the Colossians likewise—
"Wherefore if ye be dead with Christ from the rudi-
ments of the world, why, as though living in the
world, are ye subject to ordinances (Touch not; taste
not; handle not;) ...?" (Col. 2. 20–22). And he warns
them in verse 8, "Beware lest any man spoil you
through philosophy and vain deceit, after the tradition
of men ... and not after Christ."

Q. *Would you feel the same about baptism? Isn't
that also just a symbol?*

A. No, for God commands it, and it has a direct connection with the remission of sin. But if you look upon
it as a means of salvation, yes, for without the shed-
ding of blood there is no remission (forgiveness). Baptism *is* a symbol of death and resurrection (Rom. 6. 4),
but at the same time is an outward confession of an

inward work, just as we raise our hand to indicate various things that we are, or believe, etc. By baptism we are confessing publicly that we have seen ourselves to be worthy of death and fit only for burial. But we also see that we are identified by faith with Christ in His death on our behalf, and therefore we may be raised to walk in a new life of obedience to Christ. Any form of baptism is meaningless without the actual spiritual work having been done.

Q. *I thought Peter wrote to the effect that baptism saves us. That's in 1 Peter 3. 21.*

A. No. How could it? What was Peter writing about? He was writing about Noah. What saved Noah —the ark or the flood? The ark, of course; and that ark speaks of Christ. Nevertheless, the water saved and separated him from the world that was perishing. That is why Peter wrote in verse 15, "But sanctify the Lord God in your hearts." This means to separate ourselves to the Lord. Baptism, without setting ourselves apart from worldliness, to God, is mere religious sham. Baptism signifies that we are done with the worldly system, and the lust of the flesh, the lust of the eye, and the pride of life.

Q. *And Holy Communion?*

A. The Lord's table provides us with one of the simplest and most effective ways of remembering the sacrifice of the Lord Jesus on our behalf. This is the second and only other symbol commanded in the New Testament. By it we not only remember what He has done, but the remembrance of His broken body and shed blood should stir us to a full consecration to God's will, cost what it may, in devotion to Him and to bring His redemption to a lost world. But the Holy Communion was never designed to be celebrated as a superstitious conscience sedative! Set about eliminating all superstition from your Christian life and it will change your whole relationship with God and man.

THE HOLY SPIRIT

Q. *Is the baptism in the Holy Spirit the same as the new birth?*

A. No, it isn't. With a subject of this kind you can expect two extremes, and we have them. One school of thought claims that it is included in the new birth and takes place "automatically" when one is born of the Spirit. The other claims that a person is not born again until the Holy Spirit comes upon them as He came upon the disciples on the day of Pentecost.

Q. *Why is the Bible not conclusive enough to settle the matter without dispute?*

A. It is, if one is prepared to approach its revelation with humility, and not be sidetracked by private interpretations based on either a limited knowledge of the Scriptures or the limitations of one's own experience. For example, if one reads what happened to the Gentiles in Acts chapter ten and Acts chapter nineteen, in both these cases they believed, were baptized in water and the Holy Spirit came upon them, all on the same day. There is no reason why this should not still happen in this way, and it sometimes does. Now, if some people's experience coincides with what happened in those two instances, some of them become convinced that this is the only way it should happen, and, starting with such an assumption, they find "explanations" around what happend in Acts chapter eight, where they were not baptized when they believed, but only when Peter and John came down from Jerusalem and prayed for them.

Q. *If it can happen to some all on the same day, why not to all?*

A. Because not all people are the same, nor prepared to the same degree. In Acts ten and nineteen there had been tremendous preparation in both cases, seldom encountered today. As the Lord is both the only Saviour and the only Baptizer in the Holy Spirit, He holds the prerogative in His own hands. We would surely agree that it is ideal for every new convert to be baptized both in water and in the Holy Spirit on the same day that they become believers, but we neither find this in practice, nor in all cases reported in the Book of Acts. The details of what happened to the apostle Paul when he was saved are given in Acts nine, where we see that he was filled with the Spirit three days after his conversion. If we are to come to a proper understanding of what is likely to take place and the difference between new birth and the baptism in the Spirit, we must take all these instances into account.

Q. *Why could not this baptism in the Spirit also be the new birth? I mean, to quote Romans eight, "If any man have not the Spirit of Christ, he is none of His."*

A. Because there are two distinct works of the Holy Spirit which we should not confuse. The first you will find in John 1. 12, where we are told, "But as many as received Him, to them gave He power (the right) to become the sons of God, even to them that believe on His Name: which were *born* . . . of God." This is the first reference John gives in his Gospel concerning the new birth, and it reveals the exercising of a right to become something—a son of God. We cannot receive Christ apart from His Spirit; and when He enters and then indwells the new believer via this new birth, all the necessary power is there to make us sons of God.

Note that we begin as babes, as Peter says; but this indwelling Spirit is able to bring us to full growth, provided we grow by feeding on Christ, etc. The second work is referred to by the Lord Jesus Himself when in Acts 1. 8 He said, "Ye shall receive power (might), after that the Holy Spirit is come *upon* you : and ye shall be witnesses . . ." This has to do with our work for Him being effective, whereas the indwelling Spirit has to do with making us Christlike.

Q. *Are there two Spirits, then?*

A. No, definitely not. I know that some have confused the issue by teaching that at conversion we receive the Spirit of Christ, whereas at the baptism in the Spirit we receive the Holy Spirit. The terms are all right, but *He* is the same Spirit. The two titles are used synonymously in Acts 16. 6 and 7, if you consult either the RV or the NEB, as well as some other versions. Though He is the one Spirit (as taught by Eph. 4. 4), yet He carries out more than one function. To illustrate, think of a father who takes his son into business with himself, without making him a partner yet. The father would find himself fulfilling a double role, namely, father and employer. We are God's *sons* by new birth, but then need the power of the Holy Spirit to come upon us so that we may fulfil our position as *servants* also. The first relationship is permanent, whereas the second is only for the duration of our service in this life. We shall not be needing the gifts of the Spirit (which have to do with service and ministry) when we reach our eternal inheritance (see 1 Cor. 13. 8).

Q. *Are there other scriptures which back up this view?*

A. Certainly. We only need to look at the Perfect

B

Man, the Lord Himself, not as Son of God, but as Son of man. He was born of the Spirit if anyone was (Luke 1. 35) and was indwelt by the Holy Spirit for thirty wonderful years. The result was a life of purity and holiness which made Him acceptable to both God and man (Luke 2. 52). But it was not until He was baptized in water by John at Jordan that, while praying, the heavens opened and the same Holy Spirit that had always indwelt Him, now came *upon* Him. Suddenly we find the Perfect One empowered and fitted for service. Until this happened there was apparently no impact on the outside world—even the religious world; but after the Spirit came upon Him there was impact (might) everywhere. The *Son* of God had now become the *Servant* of Jehovah. As this is what happened in His humanity, we could not have a better guide to follow, and did He not say that we were to follow Him if we were to become fishers of men? In Acts two we see the same principle—saved men waiting to be baptized in the Spirit, so that they could become effective.

Q. *Would you define this baptism in the Spirit by Acts 2. 4?*

A. Though many believers do, I feel it is too limited in its content to become a definition sufficiently comprehensive for us to adopt for all Christians. Acts 2. 4 says, "There appeared unto them tongues like as of fire . . . and they were all filled with the Holy Spirit, and began to speak with other tongues, as the Spirit gave them utterance." Now read Acts 10. 46, "They heard them speak with tongues, and magnify God." Notice the differences: only Acts two speaks of tongues of fire, while Acts ten adds that they magnified God. To pick and choose would bring us into error. Then we may consult Acts 19. 6, "The Holy Spirit came on

them; and they spake with tongues, and prophesied."
Different again! I submit, therefore, that it is too risky
to take any of these three accounts as a definition, or
even all three. And it is highly likely that not all the
details were recorded, anyway, which increases our
difficulty.

Q. *I see the point, but where can one turn for an
adequate definition?*

A. What the Lord Jesus said in Acts 1. 8 should be
sufficient for us, for He said, "Ye shall receive the
power of the Holy Spirit coming upon you: and ye
shall be witnesses unto Me ... unto the uttermost part
of the earth." Here we are lifted above the sphere of
personal experience alone into the full orbit of what to
expect. To take an illustration—every space-flight
necessitates a satisfactory blast-off, when tremendous
power is needed. The thrust produces the side effects of
thunderous roars, smoke fumes, etc. All this is but the
beginning, for the blast-off is not the completed space-
flight. Similarly, there must not only be a genuine
baptism in the Spirit, when power is released, but this
baptism has an end in view—effective witness in the
way God chooses to manifest it through the person.
The baptism involves the power of the Spirit more than
the side effects of manifestations, though there should
be both. If we only look for tongues, or prophecy, or
magnifying God as the evidence of having received
"it", we are in the very real danger of missing the
power, for such utterances may be made quite apart
from the baptism in the Spirit. Demon religions, for
instance, have produced counterfeit manifestations,
and there are also other means of producing them. But
when the Lord Jesus baptizes anyone in the Spirit, His
power will come upon the believer and it is surely sen-

sible and scriptural to expect a divine utterance. No astronaut is convinced that he is "lifting off" if all the evidence he has is noise and smoke. It is the power that counts. I submit that no believer needs a "sign" that he has received the Spirit, for he will know that the Spirit is upon him. According to 1 Corinthians 14. 22, the only one who needs a sign as far as tongues is concerned is the unbeliever.

Q. *Why do some complain that since receiving the baptism they are still powerless?*

A. Each case would need examining on its own merits, of course, but this much we may establish: whenever a genuine baptism in the Spirit is received, that believer becomes charged with divine energy. The position then is like the way an electric light bulb functions: the power pours into it along one wire, but has to be released along an outgoing wire before there is light in the bulb. When the Spirit's power comes upon a believer, light appears to those in darkness as manifestations and ministries of the Spirit are allowed to function according to His will. Too many who have received this baptism are not functioning, which may be due to a variety of reasons.

Q. *What do you think it means to be a witness UNTO Jesus?*

A. I realize that the popular view of this is that being baptized in the Spirit makes witnessing for Christ more bold, easier, and possibly, more effective. I do not think such a description goes far enough, for the simple reason that many of us have known what it is to do all these things through sheer devotion and faith, and conversions have resulted. It seems to me that we only discover what is meant when we read

Acts three, to take one example. Here we see Peter and John passing by a lame beggar and doing for him what Jesus would have done had He been there in the flesh. In this sense Peter and John became witnesses *unto* Jesus.

Q. *What a challenge! Where do we fit 1 Corinthians 12. 13 into all this?*

A. Let's read it first—"For indeed we were all brought into one body by baptism, in the one Spirit, ... and that one Holy Spirit was poured out for all of us to drink." The Amplified New Testament says, "For by (means of the personal agency of) one (Holy) Spirit we were all ... baptized (and by baptism united together) into one body, and all made to drink of one (Holy) Spirit." The subject of the paragraph concerns unity of the body of Christ more than the baptism in the Spirit. It is the work of the Holy Spirit, confirmed through water baptism, to bring us all into one body, that body of which Christ is the Head. The same truth is brought out in Romans 6. 3, "Know ye not, that so many of us as were baptized *into* Jesus Christ (into union with Christ Jesus—NEB) were baptized into His death?" As we then rise from the baptismal waters, it is to walk solely in a life that is in union with Christ. The Holy Spirit accomplishes this—the baptism signifies it. That is the first part, then, of 1 Corinthians 12. 13. The latter part of the verse, however, states that it was the same Holy Spirit who was poured out (on the day of Pentecost) for all of us to drink. This time the Spirit is not the agent; it is the Lord Jesus, the sole baptizer in the Spirit, who immerses us in the Spirit.

Q. *Was the day of Pentecost the first time the disciples received the Holy Spirit?*

A. No, indeed! The first time they received the Spirit was when they were gathered together, in John 20. 22. Reading from verse 20, "Jesus repeated, 'Peace be with you!', and then said, 'As the Father sent Me, so I send you.' He then breathed on them, saying, 'Receive the Holy Spirit! If you forgive any man's sins, they stand forgiven . . .'" Some explain this by saying He was only illustrating what was going to happen on the day of Pentecost. If this is right, then the definiteness of Jesus' statement, coupled with the fact that He breathed on them there and then, would be meaningless. He did not usually do things this way. No, the Amplified New Testament makes it clear that they received the Holy Spirit on that occasion*. It was subsequent to this that they were told to wait for the historic day of Pentecost, when the Spirit now *in* them would come *upon* them.

Q. *That the day of Pentecost was historic—isn't that enough, without our having to seek a particular baptism?*

A. Look at it this way! The crucifixion was also an historic event, yet every sinner must personally and individually repent and experience the new birth. It is possible because of Calvary, but the history does not save a sinner. Similarly, each believer must be baptized with the Holy Spirit individually, in view of what happened on the day of Pentecost.

* Greek literally reads: "He breathed into them, saying, 'Receive *now* the Holy Spirit.'"

WORLDLINESS

Q. *Do I have problems! Just recently someone shook me by accusing me of being "worldly and carnal". What do you think they meant?*

A. Carnality and worldliness are much the same thing. Admittedly the terms are a bit archaic, but the problem is up-to-date. Worldliness, broadly speaking, is conforming to the generally accepted code of self-gratification, self-confidence, and trusting to security in tangible things, while ignoring God's claims upon the life. The Christian must be delivered from this completely.

Q. *But why? Aren't we supposed to make the most of life and enjoy ourselves?*

A. You'll never do it that way! If we refer to the Maker's handbook on human existence (the Bible), we find first in Romans 12. 2, "And be not conformed to this world: but be ye transformed by the renewing of your mind . . .", and then in 1 John 2. 15–17, "Love not the world, neither the things that are in the world. If any man love the world, the love of the Father is not in him. For all that is in the world, the lust of the flesh, and the lust of the eyes, and the pride of life, is not of the Father, but is of the world. And the world passeth away, and the lust thereof: but he that doeth the will of God abideth for ever." One more—Jesus prayed, "I pray not that Thou shouldest take them out of the world, but that Thou shouldest keep them from the evil. They are not of the world, even as I am not of the world" (John 17. 15, 16).

Q. *Will I ever make it? Sounds like an all-out ulti-matum!*

A. It is—and there's no way round it. Either our lives come on to the wavelength of God's will, or we choose to remain tuned to worldliness and its inevitable end. Only the former can experience salvation in Christ, for doing God's will is the outworking of salvation. If you recall that great story of Lazarus and the rich man in Luke 16, you will see that it was sheer worldliness that brought the latter to Hades. He made the fatal mistake of shutting God out of the control tower of his life and trying to make a safe landing in eternity, guided by the faulty radar of loving and living for the things of the world. He falls within the group mentioned in Psalm 17. 14, "Men of the world, which have their portion in this life, and whose belly Thou fillest with Thy hid treasure." It would have been better to be able to echo the next verse, as Lazarus certainly could—"As for me, I will behold Thy face in righteousness: I shall be satisfied, when I awake, with Thy likeness."

Q. *Hmmm! Can you give me a breakdown of the symptoms of worldliness?*

A. There are only three, and John said, in that scripture I quoted a moment ago, that they summed up *all* that is in the world. It will be of real help to consult the Amplified New Testament for these three. First of all, it translates "the lust of the flesh" as "a craving for sensual gratification". This refers to our five senses, which are connected like flash points to our bodily appetites. All our appetites were originally designed by God for our blessing and the healthy function of our bodies, but ever since sin invaded human nature they have become among our biggest enemies. They cry out

for satisfaction in a way that was not known by Adam
or Eve before they fell under the curse through disobedience. Pandering to these appetites spells certain
disaster, but controlling them—that is, placing them
under God's commandments, by His grace—brings life,
peace and, in fact, blessing. This means having to deny
ourselves, and that is why the tempter does everything
possible to turn these desires into lusts. Lust is desire
off the leash! Give way and the craving grows, and
immediately we find ourselves in bondage. The smoker
knows this craving and the way it can grip and domi-
nate one's life, but it also operates in all our appetites
in varying degrees.

Q. *Thank God that He delivered me from smoking!
Now, what's second?*

A. The lust of the eyes, or, as the Amplified puts it,
"the greedy longings of the mind". The eyes are sometimes called the windows of the soul, and it is mostly
through them that the mind gets its start into all kinds
of imaginations. The first sight of something lustful
isn't what usually does the big damage: it is rather
when we look the second time and chance becomes
deliberate choice. The first look provokes temptation,
which we have the power to reject at once, and it
should be at once. Failure to reject lets loose a quick
succession of greedy imaginations and longings which
alert all action stations for the satisfaction of our
appetites, and this is only one step away from the
committing of sin itself.

Q. *I can see that I need help right here. Is that verse
in John's Epistle an isolated one, or are there others
about the eyes?*

A. There are several, actually. The Lord Jesus referred to the lustful look having the same power as the committed sin, and went as far as advocating the plucking out of the lustful eye, rather than going to hell through it (Matt. 5. 27–29). Paul also warns us that those who practise sexual sin have no inheritance in the kingdom of God (Eph. 5. 5), while Peter speaks about some who dared partake of Christian fellowship, while "having eyes full of adultery, and that cannot cease from sin . . . cursed children: Which have forsaken the right way, and are gone astray . . ." (2 Pet. 2. 14, 15). Most sin finds its gateway to the heart through the eyes. Once past this barrier it drops like a seed into the heart and there conceives. With lust awakened it grows steadily as the conscience is slowly overcome, until it comes forth in a sinful action. The end of this plan is death, eternal death (James 1. 14–15). Listen to Achan testifying before Joshua concerning the Babylonish garment, etc., in Joshua 7. 21. "When I *saw* among the spoils . . . then I *coveted* them, and *took* them." After sin has run its course in this way, it leaves in its trail a fear of discovery, and we hear Achan conclude with the doleful admission—"They are *hid*". He thought it would satisfy once he had it all; but did it? It only brought fear, misery, discovery, shame and, finally, death.

Q. *You mentioned covetousness. Is it such a serious sin? It's pretty common these days, you know. Surely it depends on how you view it.*

A. Sin does not depend on how *we* view it! It is God who is the judge, and to commit sin is to break His divine laws. For example, in Joshua 20 God explains that there are two ways of viewing the killing of someone: on one hand, if it is premeditated in any way, or if there is hatred, it is murder; but if it is by accident, then murder is not involved. Our British law agrees with this. Because of the difference between the two, God provided protection for the accidental killer by setting up cities of refuge, but He provided nothing but judgment for the murderer. There is no such alternative with covetousness, for it is already loaded with intent and is the thought-sin of stealing. Hence, the tenth Commandment states: "Thou shalt not covet", and Ephesians 5. 5 affirms that the covetous man has no inheritance in the kingdom of Christ and of God.

Q. Well, what's the answer to covetousness?

A. When the Word hits you like this and you begin to wonder where you stand, it is always good to sit down and calmly face the relevant Bible facts and then engage in that most healthy exercise of taking stock of yourself. Worldliness became rampant in the Corinthian church and Paul wrote to them thus: "Examine yourselves, whether ye be in the faith; prove your own selves. Know ye not your own selves, how that Jesus Christ is in you, except ye be reprobates?" (2 Cor. 13. 5). In other words, is the Christian life that you profess a reality within you? If Christ indwells you, He will have displaced worldliness with His holiness. If, after profession of faith in Christ we find that we are continuing to be worldly, it may well be that Christ is not, in fact, living in us after all. Only thorough repentance, followed by saving faith, can deliver from covetousness. No act of the will is sufficient to accomplish this in you.

Q. Thanks for that. Can I go now? You've given me much that I must get through with the Lord. I need a deep heart cleansing.

A. Then take with you the third point on worldliness, namely, the pride of life, or "assurance in one's own resources, or in the stability of earthly things". To rely on your own ability or personality is worldly, just as much as putting your trust in material stability. The world is looking for security on its own terms, but not God's. Worldliness bolsters self-confidence, whereas the spiritual man puts all his confidence in God. Worldliness makes a god out of the acquisition of knowledge and urges us to become the captain of our own fate and the architect of our own lives. The spiritual man, however, abandons his sins and exercises a childlike confidence in God's ability to act as his Father. It is impossible to "love the world" and know the "love of the Father", for they cannot mix. As much of this world's "security" is reduced to financial terms, it emphasizes 1 Timothy 6. 9, 10: "But they that *will* be rich fall into temptation and a snare, and into many foolish and hurtful lusts, which drown men in destruction and perdition. For the *love* of money (covetousness) is the root of all evil: which while some coveted after, they have erred from the faith, and pierced themselves through with many sorrows." No doubt one of these was Demas, of whom Paul wrote, "Demas hath forsaken me, having loved this present world, and is departed . . ." (2 Tim. 4. 10).

THE UNFORGIVABLE SIN

Q. *I'm worried stiff! Have I committed the unfor-givable sin? I've never been so miserable.*

A. I am sure you haven't, or you would not be so concerned about it, but the best way to bring you assurance and peace is to look at the truth of the matter. Jesus promised, "And ye shall know the truth, and the truth shall make you free" (John 8. 32). Right now you are suffering from one of Satan's favourite ways of trying to bring believers into condemnation. He has several ways of accomplishing this, but few as effective as this one.

Q. *Why? Do others also suffer this kind of attack?*

A. There is hardly a Christian who is not at some time or other assaulted in this way by the arch-liar, and therefore it is just as well to apply 1 Corinthians 10. 13 to yourself without delay—"There hath no temptation taken you but such as is *common* to man . . ." Satan always tries to make you feel that your case is a special one, and in this way he is able to increase the inner tension of guilt and condemnation. But God never condemns His people—the Spirit's work is to convict, and this leads to repentance and deliverance. Condemnation leads only to bondage. If you allow this to continue, Satan will win the fight by making you impotent in the battle against his kingdom.

Q. *Please help me quickly, because I'm really worried about this. What is the truth?*

A. It falls into three divisions. The first is easy to comprehend, and we come across it in Mark three where Jesus was casting out demons and healing the sick. His ministry forced the priests and Pharisees to face up to an indisputable witness, for, if the works were being done by God through this Man, then they would be compelled to obey His message. But His message hit right at the core of their religious pretence and hypocrisy, and they could not, so they thought, afford to openly repent of their sins and follow Him. After all, they had a good outward show of religion and the people looked up to them as spiritual leaders. It is very hard for such people to have to humble themselves and repent. They tried to save face, and came to the fatal conclusion, therefore, that the motivating force in Jesus' ministry was satanic. On the ground of this false conclusion they rejected Him and His ministry.

Q. *Why would such a conclusion be so serious?*

A. Because they were saying that the Holy Spirit's power which was operative through Jesus was satanic, and this, Jesus said, was an eternal sin. By saying it, they were blaspheming against the Holy Spirit, and this is the only sin which cannot be forgiven, either in this world or the next. Jesus said that, even if people blasphemed His own name, they would be forgiven through repentance and faith; but blasphemy against the Holy Spirit can never be forgiven. This is why you should be careful never to say that the operation of any gift of the Holy Spirit is "of the devil", unless you have clear revelation from God that it is not by the Holy Spirit.

Q. *Oh my! That's done it for me, then! Once we had a friend who was prayed for and was healed, but I followed our church leaders by saying that it was of the devil.*

A. Relax! Your leaders, whoever they are, might well have hardened themselves against a clear witness of the Spirit to their own hearts, and could be in jeopardy. Because you trusted and respected their judgment, you followed their appraisal and quoted them, but I take it that this was not your own serious conclusion, resulting from hardening your heart against His Word. In that case, you sinned in ignorance, not intentionally. Next time, do not go astray like a sheep, but examine everything before God with an open heart, and seek an answer from God, according to His Word. Not all healing is from God, and of this we are not ignorant, but do not be unwise.

Q. *What relief! But you said there were three divisions. What are the other two?*

A. The second we shall consider affects true believers, but is very different from what we have just considered. It is a sin which is not forgiven on earth, but it is forgiven in heaven, thank God. Moses, that great man of God, committed such a sin. It happened when Israel was needing water for the second time in the wilderness. God told Moses to speak to the rock and it would bring forth the required stream. But, in his impatience with Israel, Moses disobeyed and struck the rock, as he had been commanded to do the previous time. Nothing happened. Moses struck it again and the water poured forth, but God would not turn away His anger in the matter, even though Moses besought Him very earnestly, later, to be allowed to enter the promised land. At that time God answered Moses, "Enough! Say no more about this" (Deut. 3. 26). When God forgives He also forgets; but again in Deuteronomy 32. 50, 51 we read, "On this mountain you shall die . . . just as Aaron . . . This is because both of you were unfaithful to me at the waters of Meribah-by-Kadesh . . ."

Q. *But why was God so hard on him?*

A. Because at that time Israel was disobeying God's commandments more and more, and, had Moses got away with this disobedience lightly, it would have been the signal for Israel to let loose into every kind of rebellion. If Moses could have found forgiveness through the usual channels, then the people would have flung themselves into iniquity, thinking that all they needed to do was to go through the forgiveness ritual and then go and sin freely again and again. The grace of God would have become sadly abused, and the precious place of forgiveness and cleansing would have been changed into nothing better than a spiritual dry-cleaning service.

Q. *Is this what John calls "a sin unto death", in 1 John 5. 16?*

A. I believe it comes in that bracket. You see, we have folk today who look upon sin very lightly, thinking that they may use that marvellous provision of confession in 1 John 1. 9 as a convenience to perpetuate their lustful desire *ad lib*. God will not tolerate it, and, whenever He chooses, He calls a halt by making an example of someone, so that the fear of God, which delivers from sin, corrects this idea sharply and delivers others who are likewise guilty. When Ananias and Sapphira died for their sin of deceit, we read that great fear came on the church. Four chapters later we also read that through "the *fear* of the Lord, and in the comfort of the Holy Ghost, (the churches) were multiplied" (Acts 9. 31). The fear of the Lord, by the way, is not something which makes one frightened of God, but which produces a deep and adequate respect for Him that makes the believer depart from the things in his life which offend God. It is such a necessary element to human existence that Solomon said, "The fear of the Lord is the principal part of knowledge" (Prov. 1. 7).

Q. *Does it mean that those who sin this "sin unto death" do not enter heaven?*

A. At least we know where we are in Moses' case. He kept on pleading his case, but God told him to say no more about it. It was in order that Israel might fear, and therefore Moses told the people that God had done it for *their* sake. Moses was not allowed to go into the promised land. But because he was denied grace for Israel's sake, it is wonderful to see how God made it up to him, for, when Jesus was transfigured on the mount before His nearest three disciples, the two who appeared from heaven were none other than Elijah and Moses. I guess, if anything, Moses preferred to visit the promised land that way, than to have entered it physically the first time! In Moses' case, Ananias and Sapphira's case, and the Corinthian church's case in 1 Corinthians 11. 30, it seems that the consequences of the sin were limited to physical death. And the purpose? In each case it was to deliver the people of God from looking carelessly on the matter of sin.

Q. *Well, it makes me think! I must confess that I was getting careless. What's the third kind?*

A. This affects those who are not saved. It is not any specific sin, but rather a steady resistance against the conviction of that sin by the Holy Spirit. When we continue to resist the truth, it loses its power on the

c

heart and also on the mind. In God's wonderful grace, He sends His Spirit to a person with every endeavour to bring him to repentance and faith. While this is happening, the Father is drawing that one to His Son, and he can come only when the Father is doing this. But if that person continues to resist conviction of sin, the point comes when the Spirit of God stops striving with him, or stops asking him to forsake his sin and seek God. Anyone dying in his sins in this condition crosses over the line into a place where it is impossible for his sins to be forgiven, for there is no second chance after death.

Q. *Does that mean that God calls a person to repentance only once?*

A. Not necessarily, thank God! God first called me to repentance when I was a lad of eight years old. I did not go through with the matter and turned my back on God. As I turned from Him, He turned from me, and another eight long years went by. During this period, I heard more sermons than I can count, but none of them registered with me, for God did not call. But friends of mine could see I was unsaved, and I believe that it was through their prayers that God called once more. I shall ever praise God for the prayers of those friends, for it was then that I responded to His call and God saved me.

Q. *Why does the call to be saved come so seldom to a person?*

A. We must realize that God's dealings with mankind are in love. Love, because of its nature, will not force another's will. Once a person says "No" to love, it can take years to rearrange a place of desperation where he will choose to call upon the Lord for salva-

tion. And when that happy moment comes, how quick
God is to respond, and His love runs to meet that person! But if people harden their hearts and reject God's
call to repentance, and die, their sins stand against
them for ever. There remains no place of forgiveness.
And hell-fire could never provide the right motive for
salvation. Salvation is essentially motivated by a desire
to come into a right relationship with God—not just to
be loosed from pain, or something akin to that. You
will see what I mean in John 2. 23, 24, ". . . many believed in His name, when they saw the miracles which
He did. But Jesus did not commit Himself unto
them . . ." They wanted healing so that they could return to their self-centred existence, and had no interest
in following Jesus. When people die in their sins, there
remains the terrifying reality of Revelation 22. 11, "He
that is unjust, let him be unjust still: and he which is
filthy, let him be filthy still." This is the point of no
return—where change becomes impossible!

HELL

Q. *Is there really such a place as hell, or is it only mythical?*

A. The spiritual world is not the same as the physical world, and our language is too limited to describe the spiritual world properly. But as sure as heaven is a place, so is hell a place. Let me illustrate the problem of words by taking some of the meanings of original Bible words, as they are used for "heaven". The Hebrew word for "heaven" means, literally, "rolling cloud", "thin cloud", "heaved up things". The Greek word *ouranus* means, "heaven, sky or air". None of these words can adequately describe heaven; in fact, they fall very short. Yet we know heaven to be a very wonderful place, for, when it was revealed to John, for example, he wrote, "I looked, and behold, a door was opened in heaven: ... and immediately I was in the Spirit: and behold, a throne was set in heaven, and One sat on the throne. And He that sat (upon the throne) was to look upon like a jasper ... and there was a rainbow round about the throne, in sight like unto an emerald ... and before the throne there was a sea of glass like unto crystal", etc. (Rev. 4.)

Now, concerning the word "hell", the Old Testament word is "sheol", meaning "the unseen state", while the New Testament word "Hades" means "the unseen world". These words indicate that hell is not only a place, but also a kind of existence. Because of the inadequacy of our English words to describe hell, we have to look further afield to complete the picture.

While Jesus was on the earth He spoke much about hell: some estimate that in the four Gospels He referred to it seven times more than He referred to heaven. Did you ever read His story of Lazarus and the rich man in Luke 16? That should be convincing enough for you!

Q. *Ah, but wasn't that only a parable?*

A. It looks more than a parable to me, but even if it was a parable, Jesus never based His parables on anything but truth. Think of His great parable of the sower and the seed. Because this was a parable, does it mean that no-one ever sows seed? Ridiculous! Jesus was one teacher who was never given to "flights of fancy", nor did He ever concoct stories which would be misleading. The details of Luke 16 are too full of horror to be discarded lightly. It was most unusual for Jesus, when using parables, to actually name one of the persons involved. I think it would be both wiser and safer to look upon it either as a factual report of a man overheard speaking in the torture of hell-fire, or at least as being based on stark reality.

Q. *Uh huh! I was told that the word "hell" is just another word for the grave, or general domain of the dead. How would you disprove that?*

A. Who's been knocking at your door, trying to sell you bogus religion? God has built some very efficient truth-protectors into the Bible, so that, when people try to avoid certain issues by reverting to the dictionary meaning of words to form the ground of their doctrine, there are other means of establishing what the truth is on the subject. Now, if the rich man entered merely the "domain of the dead", then it is abundantly clear, from what Jesus said, that it was an existence which can and should be avoided at all costs, for whatever people try to make the word "hell" mean, four times He speaks about the rich man being tormented. If you called the place "Sleepy Hollow", you could not stifle his cries for just that one drop of water to lessen his agony. Call a furnace a "domain of combustibles", but it will not lessen the power of the consuming fire which rages within it. Add to this the direct teaching of the Lord Jesus in Mark 9. 43 onwards, where He begins by saying, "And if thy hand offend thee, cut it off: it is better for thee to enter into life maimed, than having two hands to go into hell, into the fire that never shall be quenched: Where their worm dieth not, and the fire is not quenched."

Q. *But when I was learning R.I. at school we were told that "hell" in that reference is Gehenna, which is the same as a rubbish dump fire. In other words, the corruption of the body in the grave.*

A. If that's all it is, then the saint is no better off than the sinner. Also, it means that the teaching of Jesus to forsake sin was sheer drivel, for the Christian's body is as subject to corruption as is the unsaved man's. But even if you water it down to bodily corruption, how do you avoid Revelation 21. 8?—"But the fearful, and unbelieving, and the vile, and murderers, and fornicators, and sorcerers (all branches of spiritism), and idolaters, and all liars, shall have their part in the lake which burneth with fire and brimstone: which is the *second* death." The corruption of the body is only *part* of the first death; but even if you try to make it the whole of the first death, what about the second death?

Q. *That's clear! Is hell-fire in existence now, though,*

or is it only going to be at the end of things? I mean, isn't that the second death?

A. To answer your question we must return to Lazarus and the rich man. The rich man's cry was, "I *am* tormented!" Further substantiation is found in that the rich man was pleading for a message to be sent to his brothers who were still alive on the earth, so that they might repent and not share his terrible fate. Hell is not only a place, as I said before; it is an eternal condition which manifests itself in fullness once the sinner is released from the limitations of physical existence. In the same way, Lazarus was not only in a place but in a condition where eternal life blossoms forth into fullness. The true Christian is already beginning to live and enjoy eternal life here, as he has received God's "first instalment" or "down payment" (the Holy Spirit) for eternity. Similarly, sinners are already sinking on their downward course away from God and His Spirit. The demons know that hell-fire exists now, for, when Jesus cast out a legion of them in Luke 8. 31, they *"besought* Him that He would not command them to go out into the deep".

Q. *But I thought that the devil and his demons were already in hell.*

A. I wish they were, but there is a future day appointed for that, and, as far as I am concerned, it cannot come quickly enough! In verse 28 those same demons cried out to Jesus, through the possessed man, with a *loud* voice, "I beseech Thee, *torment* me not." This is the same word that the rich man used. Yes, the demons know about it, they believe it, and, what is more, they tremble (Jas. 2. 19). They know even about the appointed time for their torture, for they said in Matthew 8. 29, "... art Thou come hither to torment us before the time?" Their time is future, yet they are well aware of the existence of hell-fire in the present. Alas, after his death, the doomed sinner enters the hell-fire which was prepared for the devil and his angels.

Q. *Is that so? How soon is it before an unsaved sinner arrives in hell after his death?*

A. As far as the rich man was concerned, it took the space of two "ands". Jesus said, ". . . the rich man died, *and* was buried; *and* in hell he lifted up his eyes . . ." Those could never be physical eyes. Some accounts of death-bed scenes show clearly that for both saved and unsaved, as they are closing their physical eyes in this life, they are already opening the eyes of their spirit in the next. Remember, you are not a body. You are a spirit that is temporarily housed in a body. As soon as a human being dies, God takes immediate charge of his spirit, and all this talk about disembodied spirits hovering about, especially after a sudden accident, does not stand up to the truth of the Scriptures. On the contrary, there are plenty of demon spirits who are proficient at imitating any departed human spirit, and they have done a first-class job in deluding hosts of men and women into thinking that they were the spirits of those who had departed. Once the gates closed behind the rich man and the lock was turned, he must have been so convinced that there was no escape, that never once in the narrative did he ask to be let out.

Q. *But what if there really is no hell? I mean, could it not have been written to make us repent?*

A. After all we've already said! Let's examine your statement. First, it means that we can no longer rely on the Bible as the revelation of truth. Second, it means that God's "little confidence trick" was a bad idea, for it has not succeeded in making very many repent. Third, if there is no hell, then what happened at the cross was sheer folly and Christ was the most deluded of all fools and a deceived actor. Fourth, it means that we are not obliged to obey His commands, for there is no penalty for not doing so. Fifth, it means that righteousness is a mockery, and there are enough who think so! Can you imagine how useless our national laws would be if there were no penalties for breaking them? If God is not the centre of true justice, then where do we go from here? Sixth——

Q. *O.K., O.K.! But why did God make the penalty for sin so stiff?*

A. Because He paid that penalty Himself. Imagine if one of our judges decided that he would pay the fine for someone whom he had been obliged to condemn in the course of his duties. How would he pass sentence upon the guilty man, knowing he will pay it himself, and still retain his righteousness in the eyes of his critics? There is only one way—he must pass full sentence; otherwise he would be accused of reducing it to suit himself. Similarly, when God in His infinite grace passed sentence on the human race, knowing that He would pay that sentence Himself through the death of His own Son on the cross, He had to impose the maximum penalty upon man. This has put God's righteousness beyond criticism. And what grace! Christ died in our place, and as Psalm 88. 6, 7 says, "Thou hast laid me in the lowest pit, in darkness, in the deeps. Thy wrath (against us, not Him) lieth hard upon me, and Thou has afflicted me with all Thy waves." He paid it all, and we rejoice in the proof of that, in that He is risen from the dead. Now any sinner who accepts

Christ as the offering for his sin may pass from death to life.

Q. *Marvellous! I see it now. What else does the story of the rich man teach us about hell?*

A. More potent, probably, than anything the rich man said, was what he did not say! I have already told you that he did not ask to be let out. But neither does he claim any past good works, for he doubtless sees them in their proper light now—filthy rags! (Isa. 64. 6). During the years of my business career I often spoke to wealthy businessmen about their souls. Rich businessmen seem to have a common philosophy, which shows they often think about eternity, for many of them said to me, "Oh yes, I have sinned, but I have also done good works, helped others, and I reckon that on the Great Day I will just make it, when the balancing out is done!" But God comes down with a bang on such philosophy when He declares that these good works are only filthy rags. Next, the rich man does not claim that God has treated him unfairly or unjustly. After all, he was not a murderer, or an adulterer, or a thief; he probably lived a secluded life of luxurious decency. Mind you, he had not believed and had quietly shut God out of his self-centred life. Possibly, in hell, he was made aware of some words in Proverbs 22. 22, 23, ". . . neither oppress the afflicted in the gate: for the Lord will plead their cause, and spoil the *soul* of those that spoiled them." Never does the rich man utter the name of God in that awful place, for even though this is the only name on earth which has eternal hope, he must know there is no such hope in hell. The soul that lives without God dies without God.

Q. *Would God have saved him, do you think, if he HAD repented?*

A. There is no possibility of repentance in hell, even if he knew exactly why he was there. Knowledge of sin does not produce repentance, for repentance is a gift from God by the Holy Spirit, but there is no such work of the Holy Spirit in hell. You will notice that, although the rich man desires the repentance of his brothers on earth, there is not a word about his own. You would think that the interminable suffering would make him cry out, "O God, I have sinned. I am sorry I have sinned. Please forgive me!" But no, not a word like that. Because there is no work of the Holy Spirit in hell, there is no repentance; because there is no repentance, there is no forgiveness or salvation. How important, therefore, are the words of Peter in Acts 3, 19, "Repent ye therefore, and be converted, that your sins may be blotted out . . ."

Q. *Never thought of that! What do you think about his request to let someone rise from the dead and testify of hell to living men and women?*

A. Waste of time! Just imagine if someone arranged a meeting, announcing that he had risen from the dead and would testify of conditions in hell. We would very likely try to have him certified. You see, deep down we all know that there is no escape from hell. But now consider this: there *was* one that rose from the dead, even Jesus. He knows what is behind the veil of death, yet you even queried the veracity of the Luke 16 narrative. Folk don't want to believe that He rose from the dead, though he was seen by over 500 witnesses who not only saw Him but heard Him, and some even touched Him (sufficient evidence of reality for any psychologist). But who will believe the report, undeniable after two millenniums of history? Only those who are ready to believe the word of the prophets, as Jesus Himself said. Faith comes by *hearing*, and hearing the Word of God, because it is through that chosen agency that the Holy Spirit does most of His work.

Q. *I think this chat together has done something new for me, especially with regard to others.*

A. I am so glad. The account of the rich man was not given by Jesus to satisfy curiosity. It reveals deep truths which only the sentimental and wilful choose to avoid. And, as you have just said, it should awaken tremendous concern in the heart of any believer for the lost sinner. Therefore, before concluding this great subject, let me draw your attention to Luke 16, where it says that Lazarus was "desiring to be fed with the crumbs which fell from the rich man's table", but was refused, apparently. Do you remember what the Canaanite woman said to Jesus one day? Hear these words—"Truth, Lord: yet the dogs eat of the crumbs which fall from their masters' table" (Matt. 15. 27). As a believer, you are sitting at the Master's table, eating the bread of life. Through revelation of the saving Word, you have entered into eternal life. You have been made rich in Christ. Can you deny crumbs to the needy ones all around you? Paul said, "Woe is unto me, if I preach not the gospel!" (1 Cor. 9. 16), and, "If our gospel be hid, it is hid to them that are lost" (2 Cor. 4. 3). The Christian's responsibility to spread the good news to lost sinners is tremendous. Could it be that there are souls now in this flame, tormented day and night, because we did not communicate the command to them to repent?

PREDESTINATION

Q. *This predestination business leaves me cold and confused. Are we really robots?*

A. Something must be wrong with the way you are thinking, because truth does not have such an effect on people. But don't be downhearted, because this subject is not an easy one to sort out and many share your feelings. However, it is a subject well worth investigating so that we can understand it and be helped by it. If we think that it means our behaviour is irrevocable, we run into the danger of accusing God for the sinful fall of man in Eden, and for the consequences it brought on the human race. If this were the case, commandments to repent would become illogical and the sacrifice of Christ on the cross meaningless, except to a God who gloats over our humiliation. Conversely, if everything were left to man's will, be sure our wills are such that the last thing we would do would be to humble ourselves and repent. We love our independence too much to want to give it up, even to God. As you might expect, a hot subject like this has two strong extremes, and, as always, the truth lies somewhere between them.

Q. *That's a comfort, but what about someone like Judas Iscariot? He had to betray Jesus because it was prophesied. Could something like that happen to me?*

A. Prophecy did not make it happen. Prophecy never does make it happen, but foresees what will happen (in cases of judgment) if sin is persisted in. When the king of Nineveh heard the prophecy that his city would be destroyed by God's judgment in forty days, he called for national repentance, and the city was saved. If you use it the right way, prophecy of judgment can be an 'early warning system' to help you change your ways in time. Mark says about the Judas case: "Jesus answered . . . The Son of Man will die as the Scriptures say he will; but how terrible for that man who will betray the Son of Man! It would have been better for that man if he had never been born!" (Mark 14. 21). God not only knew the course events would take, but issued this powerful warning to the man who was preparing his own downfall. Alas, the warning was not heeded. If Judas had been born for the specific task of betraying Jesus, God could hardly say that it would have been better not to have been born at all, for the will of God is good, acceptable and perfect (Rom. 12. 2).

Q. *Fair enough, but what do you do with strong words such as you find in Ephesians 1. 4?*

A. You have to see them in two contexts: the immediate context of the passage and the general context of Bible truth. In other words, first you must understand them in their setting; second, you must adjust them to the general tenor of truth on this subject as found in the whole of the Scriptures. Let's read your verse: "In Christ he chose us before the world was founded, *to be* dedicated, *to be* without blemish in his sight, *to be* full of love; and he has destined (predestinated, in AV) us—such was his will and pleasure—*to be* acceptable as his sons through Jesus Christ, in order that the glory of his gracious gift, so graciously bestowed on us in his Beloved, might redound to his praise" (verses 4–6). Verse 11 continues, "In Christ indeed we have been given our share in the heritage, as was decreed in his design whose purpose is everywhere at work." There are two main things to observe in these verses: first, the words "in Christ", and second, the purpose of his selection. The words "in Christ" signify that it was more a case of our being chosen *in* Him, than chosen to *be* in Him. That is, because God chose Christ, He has also chosen all that would be united to Him. For instance, I may make a decision about one of my sons, upon whom I wish to bestow a special favour, and I decide, "Whoever marries my son will be regarded as a special daughter and receive particular presents, etc." This does not mean that I have chosen my son's bride for him, but it means that whoever falls in love with him, and he decides to marry, will be accepted by me and receive what I have promised. Because of my delight in my son, I accept her in him, and announce that fact before I know who she is. (The difference with God is that He knows all.)

Q. Oh! Is that how God got the "whosoever believes in him" into John 3. 16, because he had made his choice through Jesus before the world was made?

A. We're getting there. The second thing about His destiny is with regard to His specific purposes for the believer. That is, not an irrevocable choice made at random, but a distinct purpose with the one who becomes a believer, namely, to be without a mark and full of love, and to receive our share of the heritage, etc. You might say, continuing my allegory, that whoever marries my son will be given the benefits of the best culture at my expense, so that she is a credit to the family, and will receive her part of the will in due time, co-heir with my son. The advantage that God the Father has is that through His limitless knowledge He already knows who is to become the bride of His Son, and salvation is from Him, through the Son.

Q. *I'm getting interested now! Are there other references to substantiate what you say?*

A. Yes, there are, but please remember that we are still considering the purpose of His choice. We shall look now at 1 Peter 1. 2, "You were chosen as a result of God the Father's own purpose, *to be* made a holy people by his Spirit, and *to obey* Jesus Christ and *be made* clean by his blood." In the next chapter, verse 9, he writes, "But you are the chosen race, the King's priests, the holy nation, God's own people, chosen *to proclaim* the wonderful acts of God, who called you from darkness into his marvellous light." In both quotes you will see that the choosing had to do with His purpose *with* us, and not the individual selection *of* us. We are chosen to be holy, to proclaim His acts, etc. We might as well add Ephesians 2. 10 here: "For we are his workmanship, created in Christ Jesus for good works, which God prepared beforehand, that we should walk in them." Again it has to do with our spiritual walk rather than our random selection.

Q. *Why do you say "random selection"? You have said this twice now.*

A. Because if the foreknowledge of God had nothing to do with the fact that He chose those whom He knew would respond to His call, then the selection must have been at random. Remember that God has revealed His will for *all* mankind by declaring, "God ... who desires all men to be saved and to come to the knowledge of the truth" (1 Tim. 2. 4). And, "It is not that the Lord is slow in fulfilling his promise ... but is very patient with you, because it is not His will for any to be lost, but for all to come to repentance" (2 Pet. 3. 9). One more—"As for the times of ignorance, God has overlooked them; but now he commands mankind, all men everywhere, to repent . . ." (Acts 17. 30). These three scriptures would be meaningless drivel if God had decided from the beginning who would be saved, and would reduce the salvation of sinners to the level of a lottery.

Q. *I take it that you are not impressed with the doctrine of the perseverance of the saints.*

A. That depends. If you mean that the saints are required to persevere to the end—yes; but if you mean it in the sense that the "elect" persist to the end, no matter what, then it is difficult to reconcile that with certain scriptures, for while God says in Philippians 1. 6, "And so I am sure of this: that God, who began this good work in you, will carry it on until it is finished in the Day of Christ Jesus", He also says in 2 Peter 1. 10, "So then, my brothers, try even harder to make God's call and his choice of you a permanent experience, for if you do so you will never fall away (which means you can): in this way you will be given the full right to enter the eternal kingdom of our Lord and Saviour Jesus Christ." The NEB puts it like this, "Exert yourselves to clinch God's choice and calling of you." Coupled with this are several stern warnings, notably in the book of Hebrews, that our salvation has a condition of continuance (not a guarantee of it), and whoever endures to the end will be saved. This should not be interpreted as salvation by works, but the working out of continual faith in experience.

Q. *Would you not believe in God's irresistible grace, then?*

D

A. While it is true that God can have mercy on whoever He chooses to have mercy, it is quite another matter to accept that mercy. Love never forces its way. Sad to say, we have the power to frustrate God's grace, and He warns us: "Working together with him, then, we entreat you not to accept the grace of God in vain. For he says, 'At the acceptable time I have listened to you, and helped you on the day of salvation.' Behold, now is the acceptable time; behold, now is the day of salvation" (2 Cor. 6. 1, 2). Jesus made it plain that people could only come to the Son when the Father drew them (this is the "acceptable time"). There is an appointed time for God's grace to come to a sinner. But we have the power to refuse it. Remember the rich young ruler? Remember the injunction not to harden our hearts? The call goes to many, but only few are finally chosen. Is God such a tease that He calls those whom He knows have no chance of salvation? What a libel!

Q. *Yes, but wasn't Pharaoh raised up to be an example of judgment, or something? Doesn't it say that God hardened his heart? What hope did he have?*

A. We had better read it: "For Scripture says to Pharaoh, 'I have raised you up for this very purpose, to exhibit my power in my dealings with you, and to spread my fame all over the world.' Thus he not only shows mercy as he chooses, but also makes men stubborn as he chooses" (Rom. 9. 17, 18). From that you can see the purpose, to make him an example to all men of history, so that we might not play fast and loose with God's grace and judgment like he did. And yet, if you read the story closely, watch God's long-suffering with him. For the first five plagues, Pharaoh willingly hardened his own heart, which was tantamount to shaking his fist in the face of God. Many think they can do the same today. They would be wiser to learn from Pharaoh, so that God can have mercy on them, for, after the five occasions, *then* God hardened his heart. Solemn thought! No one ever begins as a compulsive rejector of Christ, but can become one, and this is the warning.

Q. *What did Jesus mean by saying that all the Father gave Him would come to Him?*

A. It comes from John chapter six, verses 37, 38, 40, 44, 45, and we should look it up. "Every one whom my Father gives me will come to me. I will never turn away anyone who comes to me. For I have come down from heaven to do the will of him who sent me, not my own will ... For this is what my Father wants: that all who see the Son and believe in him should have eternal life; and I will raise them to life on the last day ... No one can come to me unless the Father who sent me draws him to me ... The prophets wrote, 'All men will be taught of God.'" The importance of what this reveals should be carefully noted, for when the Lord Jesus came to this world He did nothing of Himself. Even when He asked the twelve who He was and Peter confessed that He was the Christ, Jesus immediately stated that flesh and blood had not revealed this to him (Jesus was flesh and blood at the time), but that it was His Father in heaven. This is the way we should work for God, too. Evangelism can be too much of human persuasion and human decision, whereas salvation is only of and from God (see John 1. 13). Jesus accepted no one unless the work done in them was of God, and we will have to learn to work this way if we are going to avoid so many failures. This is why Jesus did not press the young ruler, though He loved that young man. Too-eager counsellors sometimes persuade people they are saved before the work is done from above. It is better for the convert to receive the witness of the Spirit themselves. That is the true case of new birth.

Q. *I've one more. It's that bit in Romans about Jacob and Esau and their election. I am thoroughly nonplussed by it.*

A. It's in Romans 9. 11–13. "In order that God's selective purpose might stand, based not upon men's deeds but upon the call of God, she was told, even before they were born, when they had as yet done nothing, good or ill, 'The elder shall be servant to the younger'; and that accords with the text of scripture, 'Jacob I loved and Esau I hated.' " The rest of the chapter ought to be read, but cannot be quoted here. On one hand it must be realized that God is not obliged to do anything for any human being, for all have rebelled against Him, but He has declared that He will have mercy on whoever He chooses to have mercy. Furthermore, He delights in mercy. What we must try to establish is whether His choice on whom to show mercy is just willy-nilly, or based upon some responsible factors that govern His choice. The passage says that works are not the deciding factor, and this is certainly true, for Jacob was a twister. However, it was the same Jacob who wholeheartedly sought the Lord and found grace when he refused to let the Angel go until he blessed him! Esau was a fine sporting type, but when the crunch came he sold his birthright for the sake of satisfying his hunger. God wrote this epitaph on his action, "Thus Esau despised his birthright" (Gen. 25. 34). We have seen that God wills not the death of any; we must also understand that He who commands us to have no respect of persons, has none Himself. We are left, therefore, with only one thing, and that is the foreknowledge of God. At one time the promise was there for Esau, but he sold it. It became Jacob's, not because of his clever deal against Esau, but because it was ratified when he broke through with God at Jabbok (Gen. 32. 29). And what happened to these two lads is the alternative that faces every person that ever hears the good news of the gospel of Jesus Christ.

JOY

Q. *Today I need joy! How do you get it when you're feeling as flat as I do?*

A. Joy is not a separate commodity, but is the result of certain other things being right. As you cannot go into a chemist's shop and buy health, for health results from the right functioning of the body, so you cannot acquire joy without the proper function of certain spiritual factors. Joy is part of the fruit of the Holy Spirit; and as healthy fruit needs a healthy tree, so real joy requires that we allow the Holy Spirit to function properly in our lives.

Q. *But weren't the disciples of Jesus suddenly filled with great joy, at the end of Luke 24? Wasn't it something that just descended upon them? I pray for joy like that but never get it!*

A. No, it was not something which dropped on them from outer space. If you look again you will see that Jesus had just been taken up from before them, having given them a mighty promise to look forward to. Then an angel had appeared to them and told them that He was coming back again. The combination of these two wonderful things let loose a fountain of joy within them that, coupled with intercession in Acts chapter one, prepared them adequately for the day of Pentecost.

Q. *Aren't you putting too much importance on joy?*

A. It was you who wanted it! Let the Bible answer

your question from Nehemiah 8. 10, "... for the *joy* of the Lord is your strength," from which we deduce that a joyless Christian is a weak Christian as well as a bad advertisement of God's grace. That's very important, but read Deuteronomy 28. 47, 48, "Because thou servedst not the Lord thy God with joyfulness, and with gladness of heart, ... therefore thou shalt serve thine enemies which the Lord shall send against thee, in hunger, and in thirst, ... and He shall put a yoke of iron upon thy neck, until He have destroyed thee." What happened to Israel physically as a penalty for joylessness, takes place spiritually with Christians, for joylessness makes us dry and weak, and we find our spiritual lives shrivelling up.

Q. *Oh! I did not realize it was so important to God! How do I get this joy, then?*
A. God has provided four ways in which we can have not only joy but what He calls "fullness of joy". Any order will do, but let us begin with 1 John 1. 4, "These things write we unto you, that your joy may be full." Not only does this refer immediately to what is written in that chapter, but the whole Word of God has been written to fulfil this purpose for us. The Bible contains riches that fill us with joy when they are appropriated. Psalm 119. 162 declares, "I rejoice at Thy word, as one that findeth great spoil." Jeremiah adds (15. 16), "Thy word was unto me the joy and rejoicing of mine heart." The Lord Jesus added this about His words: "These things have I spoken unto you, that My joy might remain in you, and that your joy might be full."

Q. *Sounds great! But how do you get the Bible to do that for you? I confess—I don't!*

A. The secret is to *feed* on the Word. That means to meditate on it, think around it and pray over it, until its truth lights up your heart and changes your life to conform to it. Many Christians pay a lot of attention to reading their Bible, or studying it from various angles; but there is no substitute for feeding on it. Reading and studying it will give you knowledge in your mind, whereas feeding on it will produce truth in your inner man. It will mean having to put time aside to wait upon the Teacher, the Holy Spirit (see 1 John 2. 27), so that He may take of the things of Christ and reveal them to you. Nothing is more precious to a believer than to have these things revealed to him, and to partake of them, and this experience fills the heart with joy. A word from God every day, given personally by Him to you, is enough to rejoice your heart to the full for the whole day.

Q. *I have known snatches of this. Can I have it daily, though?*

A. It took me one year to learn the secret of this daily reality, but you need not be as slow as I was. Remember, it is a spiritual exercise; God does not play up to the feelings, but feeds the heart or inner man. If received daily, it will produce fullness of joy daily. But if there is a day when the Word seems to yield nothing, then there are other ways, and the second is found in John 16. 24: "Ask, *and receive*, that your joy may be full." To keep on praying, without receiving the answer, will have the reverse effect and depress you. But when the secret of faith is learned, and you realize that the great Eternal God is paying attention to your cries, it fills the heart with joy. To have a God who answers is the lifeblood of our Christian testimony, for He is no idol.

Q. *I don't understand you. What do you mean by that?*

A. When, without dispute, it is God who has done something for us, we have then had personal experience of His intervention and thus have a story to tell. A testimony is nothing less than that. What God has done so fills the heart with joy that you just have to tell it! An elder of a certain church in a European country once requested prayer for healing. His life was threatened by cancer of the throat and he had been lined up by the specialist for a major operation during the following week. At his request, we prayed for him according to the four conditions listed in James 5. 14–16. At the time neither he nor we felt anything, and although we believed, our joy was quite dormant. But when, in due time, he appeared before the specialist, he was thoroughly examined and found to be completely whole. When news of this answer to prayer reached us we were filled with great joy, and still are every time the story is told. Zacharias was told that he and Elizabeth would be filled with joy and gladness (Luke 1. 14). In the original the word "gladness" means "much leaping", and I must confess we felt just the same! But in an English city, a paralysed lad from the same denomination was prayed for by some young men from his assembly. They used the same promise in James but were not careful to obey all its conditions. They prayed, but there was no answer, no miracle—and neither was there any joy. It is essentially the answer to prayer that fills with joy. Got it now?

Q. *Clearly! This is what I need. What else?*

A. Peter, preaching on the day of Pentecost, said, "Thou hast made known to me the ways of life; Thou

shalt make me *full of joy* with Thy countenance" (Acts
2. 28). He was quoting Psalm 16. 11, which says, "In
Thy presence is fullness of joy." Look at it this way. If
Jesus suddenly appeared to you in the flesh during the
next time you are waiting upon Him in prayer and
meditation, how would you feel? If He stood there like
any other person, to answer your questions, guide and
direct you, show you the way of life and receive your
worship, how would you feel?

Q. *Feel? I'd go mad with excitement and tell everyone about it. Why do you ask?*

A. Because it can be just like that, except for His
physical presence. Many of us *hope* that one day God
will do or say something, but *faith* recognizes His
actual presence and establishes and enjoys His presence
at once. God longs that we experience this reality of
fellowship and worship and even says that He seeks
such to worship Him (John 4. 23). We desperately need
this reality of His presence. Faith must reckon with it
and begin to commune with the living God, not by
some "airy-fairy" superstition but by real faith. That is
why the Word says, "He that comes to God must believe that *He is*." God lives only in the present. A personal audience with any great reigning monarch, once
the first reactions of awe and fear had subsided, would
fill us with joy, wouldn't it?

Q. *You're not kidding! But how in the world ...?
It's no good bluffing yourself. You must KNOW that
God is there; otherwise you're only putting on an act.*

A. True! There's no place in Christianity for superstition. But there is every need for faith. God is a Spirit,
and we must separate the spiritual from the physical. If
you desire fellowship with someone, you need to meet

them personally. If you desire fellowship with God, you need to meet Him spiritually. Your feet usually get you into the physical presence of another human being. It is faith that gets you into the presence of the living God! I know it's tough at the start, but be encouraged by the fact that Jesus said, even to His disciples, "O fools, and slow of heart to believe . . ." The Scripture tells us that God fills the heaven and the earth (Jer. 23. 24). It is true and we need to believe it, and act upon it; otherwise we are little better than the atheist, and are heading for agnosticism. God has stated clearly, "Draw nigh to God, and He will draw nigh to you" (Jas. 4. 8). We'd better believe it, *for He does*!

Q. *I must confess failure in that regard. Is there anything else?*
A. I've given you three ways, and there are probably other ways of receiving this fullness of joy, but let me take you to one more. John said, "I have no greater joy than to hear that my children *walk* in truth" (3 John 4).

Q. *What an anti-climax! It's not even centred on the Lord!*
A. This is no anti-climax, as I hope you will live to see. I used to think, too, that John must have become somewhat confused when he wrote that verse, for surely the greatest joy is centred in Christ. But look here—did you ever read what Paul wrote in Galatians 4. 19?—"My little children (new converts), of whom I travail in birth again until Christ be formed in you . . ." To this should be added that other scripture which states that, after the great pains of travail for physical birth, a mother forgets her pain because of the "joy

that a man is born into the world" (John 16. 21). It is always a great joy to see God answer prayer and bring a person into the kingdom of God by new birth. But here is something greater than that! Neither Paul nor John could rest until such a person was walking in the truth. When you see all that Christ has done for you being reproduced in the person whom you have led to Christ, it fills you with a joy that cannot be declared. When Mary knew that she was to give birth to the Messiah, she was filled with such joy that she exclaimed, "My soul doth magnify the Lord, and my spirit hath rejoiced in God . . ." (Luke 1. 46, 47). And when you see Christ formed in another, through your instrumentality and travail, it produces a similar flood of joy.

Q. *Thank you for these four things. Can I have them NOW?*

A. Begin at once. It might take a time for these things to take shape, but any of them singly can fill you with joy. Two of them will make you overflow! All four of them will make you "burst at the seams", except that your capacity will then expand accordingly!

SEPARATION

Q. *Hey, where can I find a cloister?*

A. Do you know what a cloister is? In any case, why do you want to shut yourself away in a corner for the rest of your life? What is it that you cannot face up to? Out with it!

Q. *Well, seriously, I have a big desire to live for God only. I have been reading what Paul said—"Come out from among them and be ye separate." Where do I start?*

A. Ah, now I understand you. Separation is not so much a matter of geography as it is a way of living. We could lay a foundation stone to our subject by referring to the words of the Lord Jesus in John 17. 15, "I pray not that Thou shouldest take them out of the world, but that Thou shouldest keep them from the evil." Many appear to have misunderstood what the Bible says about separation, and you are heading that way now. The Bible expression, "the world", can mean either the world of men or the system of worldliness. We are to separate from the second so that we can reach the first; otherwise we are likely to eke out our lives in a clique, instead of letting them make an impact on the world for God and His glory.

Q. *Steady! What could be better than separating your life to live for God alone? Won't we be doing that in heaven?*

A. Well, we're not in heaven yet, but in any case you have probably not realized that it says in Revela-

tion 22. 3, ". . . and His servants shall serve Him."
Heaven will not be taken up with lessons on the harp
and prayer meetings, but with worship and divine purpose. It is true that some Christians have been called to
a life of intercession, but intercession means serving
God with prayer that prevails for others. If you just
shut yourself away in a corner, you might find yourself
serving yourself instead of God. For example—mar-
riage is a sacred relationship, but what would you
think of a wife who wished to be chained to her hus-
band day and night, admiring and following him
everywhere, while ignoring family and social responsi-
bilities? Of course, it is just as bad to become so involved with service that we ignore the worship and
fellowship with God for which we were primarily
made.

Q. *What about old Anna the prophetess when Jesus
was born? Wasn't she just shut away in the temple,
waiting upon God as I want to?*

A. Let's read what Luke 2. 37, 38 records about Anna
—"a widow of about 84 years, which departed not
from the temple, but served God with fastings and
prayers night and day . . . and spake of Him to all them
that looked for redemption in Jerusalem." She was
aged and must have known God in a very intimate
way, but was on the job to the end. It would help if we
understand that God runs everything, basically, on two
laws. The first is that we love Him with all our heart,
soul, mind and strength. This is what you want to do.
Fair enough. But the second is like the first (said Jesus)
and is that we love our neighbour as ourselves. This is
what you must be careful to include. Because of the
human instinct to specialize, many Christians concen-
trate on loving God and forget the neighbour, while

many in the world expend great energy on helping the neighbour and forget God. We need both laws, and in the right order.

Q. *Why did Paul spend three years in the Arabian desert, or somewhere, alone?*

A. It was necessary for Paul, as it is for us, to be equipped by God with an anointing of the Holy Spirit, before he could be effective for God in the world. By all means shut yourself away for a limited period, so that you may emerge with divine authority to reach men and women for Christ. When God saved Paul, He did not say that He would make Paul a statue in the church, to be admired by all the saints, but said, "He is a chosen vessel unto Me, to bear My name before the Gentiles, and kings, and the children of Israel." As soon as Paul was equipped with revelation and an anointing from above, you do not find him circumventing ecclesiastical buildings for the rest of his life, chanting spiritual dirges. You will find him preaching in synagogues and markets, Mars Hill and other places where people gathered. He was thrown into prison after prison, and in one case sang songs which shook a prison and converted its jailor. He mixed with sinners everywhere, bearing witness to this wonderful Jesus who had transformed his life—his everyday life! But you do not find him sinning with sinners. Was not the Lord also maligned by religious humbugs because He ate with sinners? He did not partake of their sin, but was out among them and was finally crucified on the city's hill of execution, not in a cloister. The cross was planted out in the public view—not hidden in the shadows of a synagogue. He died between two common thieves and never lay in state in a cathedral. Men meant everything to Him—institutions nothing!

Q. *Revolutionary, hey!*

A. If that is a revolutionary—yes! God hates the "holier than thou" attitude we often take against others (Isa. 65. 5). We would never admit it, but we certainly act like it. Whenever there is an evangelistic campaign or special meeting to win souls, many Christians say they do not have a single unsaved friend they can invite. It seems we have forgotten that we also were once lost sinners ourselves. While we talk a lot about doing God's will, inside the walls of our church, we forget, like the Pharisees did before us, the weightier matters of judgment and mercy. Instead of using opportunities to witness for our Master where it might cost us ridicule and mocking, we prefer to separate ourselves from "these vile sinners" and sit at home with slippered feet, listening to our favourite choir sing "Go ye into *all* the world" on our record-players (so amplified that the neighbours are aggravated).

Q. *You're preaching now. What's your view of Bible schools? Would you call them cloisters?*

A. Let me finish that sermon first! Jesus once said to His disciples, "Ye call Me Lord, but do not the things which I say" (Luke 6. 46). It was He who commanded us to love our neighbour as ourselves. We must certainly separate ourselves from our neighbours' sinful ways; otherwise we shall hardly be able to show him the difference that Christ has made to our lives, but our Lord Jesus is essentially Lord for everyday life. Ephesians five and six will show us that He does not stop in the church building when the services are over, but goes home with His people, and to their places of work, to be Lord of every detail. Was He not a carpenter Himself at one time? His great mission is essentially to people—people in need of His healing, saving and transforming power. As for Bible schools, I believe they should be seen purely from the viewpoint of adequate study preparation for the worker, but never as a cloister, nor as a standard of spiritual attainment. God's dealings with Gladys Aylward are a rebuke to the way we place education before heavenly anointing.

Q. *How do you relate this matter of separation to the Christian when it comes to dancing, for example?*

A. I thought it would have been clear to you by now. On the one side, dancing falls very clearly into the category of worldliness, particularly with its connection to the lust of the flesh. If we are to obey the word in Romans 12. 2, "Be not conformed to this world ... that ye may prove what is that good, and acceptable, and perfect, will of God", then that should settle it for any Christian. But, at the same time, we cannot ignore the fact that those who do these things are among the very people whom we are commanded to reach with the gospel of Jesus Christ. We need to separate from *it* so that we can win *them*.

Q. *Would you attend a dance to do so?*

A. Most certainly I would, provided I was given permission to tell them, publicly or privately, about Jesus.

Q. *You've obviously done this. How did you go about it?*

A. We ask for permission to take the platform for fifteen or thirty minutes, or to move freely among the dancers and talk to them about Jesus when they come to sit down. On one occasion, the orchestra quit by

E

arrangement and we were given thirty minutes to sing
and preach. We used our music, for many of them are
sick of theirs! Then the story of the cross is that which
carries most impact. We have often done this in
Sweden, and were very graciously accepted. In West
Berlin, three of us went into a dance hall for an hour,
not to dance but to seek an opportunity to tell someone about eternal salvation, and had a marvellous
opportunity to speak for a long while to the leader of
the band. He said, knowing I once used to lead a jazz
band, "Maybe what you fellows have found is right, but
I can tell you that we have found no answer here." In
Stockholm we were granted the platform for fifteen
minutes in one of Europe's hottest teenage dancing
dives. They listened intently. In London, a Baptist
minister and I went to the local dance hall after church
one Sunday night. They would not allow us on the
platform, but let us mix freely with the dancers. It was
great! Every one of them was willing to listen. All but
one disliked the crashing disharmony and were seeking
for an answer to life.

Q. *Not everyone is fitted for such work, but I see the
point. How would you view my firm's annual Christ-
mas dinner? I wouldn't go, because they drink so
much at such functions.*

A. And your workmates probably think your religion *is* restricted to a cloister! You could have
accepted your employer's courtesy and used the occasion wisely as an opportunity for gossiping the gospel,
as they say. When our Lord was accused of "eating
and drinking with sinners", note that His critics were
the religious type, not the sinners, and sinners are
quick to fault a man of God for irregular behaviour. As
to what He ate and drank, this would most certainly be

governed by obedience to the Word. All His life was in complete keeping with the Scriptures. It was this very factor which would not only cause Him to eat and drink so as to glorify God, but would also take Him to where sinners who needed Him were. While the Bible commands, "Let your moderation be known unto all men" (Phil. 4, 5). it also warns "Wine is a mocker, strong drink is raging: and whosoever is deceived thereby is not wise" (Prov. 20. 1). As these are probably your convictions, you will find that the taking of a soft drink often opens up very useful conversations, but it is never wise to become embroiled in an argument about the virtues of abstinence. Rather, the opportunity should be taken to talk about Jesus to fellow-employees and guests. Eating and drinking with sinners in the way your Master did involves us in neither personal sin nor compromise. By the way, don't your workmates call you "parson"?

Q. *How did you know?*
A. Because they think you are isolated from them in your church or chapel. We are to separate from the unclean thing so that we can win the unclean person. A friend and I were once on a sea voyage from Cape Town to London and got busy spreading the gospel among the 650 passengers as much as we could, from chair to chair, and by Sunday meetings in the ship's lounge. We did not think we had accomplished much until we heard how angry the ship's purser was with us. This was the height-of-the-season trip, and he told a person we knew that our witnessing had sharply cut his liquor sales. I am so glad we did not decide to hide our Christianity in our cabin and hold secret "holy" sessions down there.

Q. *Any suggestions for reaching the rebel types who hang about in gangs?*

A. If riding on their bikes with them will open their hearts to the gospel, that is fine. But to fetch their favourite music into the house of God, so as to attract them in, is not the way. The gospel never presents a hero, nor talented stars, but presents Christ crucified, with no trappings. We are instructed to present Him to sinners, lifted up on a cross of shame, the innocent dying for the guilty, and told that this would be sufficient to draw all men to Him, including the rebel types. The Christian need never imitate anyone but Christ, and this is surely what the drifting crowds are waiting to see.

LIFE'S PURPOSE

Q. *What do you think about these youth demonstra-tions these days?*

A. They can be useful, if the young people show that they know how to steer their boat in this storm of social upheaval. The gale that is blowing could take them towards their greatest destination, provided they show skilful seamanship. If not, these "demos" could be the beginning of the greatest disaster the world has ever witnessed. It seems to me that young people today have it within their power to save or destroy civiliza-tion.

Q. *I'm surprised. I thought you would have opposed it hotly, like most of your generation.*

A. Be kind. We who are older are not as knowledge-able, perhaps, as young people today, but at least we have experience. We don't always say what we think, for many of us have learned that there is often a better way. But one thing I must readily admit: the great bulk of my generation has missed the real purpose of life and has settled for something which is much less. Not having found the answer, we have accepted a seda-tive! Mind you, not all of us have missed the way. My generation has known an increase of knowledge which dwarfs previous discovery, and it is my generation that put the first men on the moon. Spiritually, too, my generation has prepared the way for a moving of God which is already in evidence. But in the main we have failed to discover life's purpose, and, as this is evident to young people, they have revolted against our acceptance of the status quo. This could really lead somewhere! The troubling thing is that so many young people confuse true liberty with licence.

Q. *What do you mean?*
A. Well, for example, they desire to throw moral restraint overboard, for they feel it restricts their liberty. What they are not realizing is that this "liberty" leads to sickness, depravity and bondage—which other generations have discovered by experience. Why don't young people learn by our experience and pave a better road? They think the Ten Commandments are outdated, but we discovered to our cost that they dare not be ignored.

Q. *Don't you agree with the "new morality", then?*
A. Of course not, for there is no such thing! You can have neither a new morality nor an old morality. It is an eternal thing, and never becomes outdated. If you want to know what this "new morality" is, it is nothing more or less than an excuse for the old human plague of immorality. Do it now—pay heavily later!

Q. *But many things need to be overthrown. Don't you agree?*
A. Readily! But go about it in the right way. This will surprise you, but let me say now that the best way is not via anarchism, but via submission. Not submission to evil, but a learning of submission to God first, and then to men for His sake. Sounds complicated, and even defeatist, but let's pursue it, for its strength is unequalled. Our problem is not old people, restrictive laws, bad conditions, or the many obvious inequalities. Man's biggest problem is resident within

himself. For example, the difficulty is not to get rid of that great Commandment, "Thou shalt not commit adultery", but to learn the secret of overcoming the power of lust. The need is not higher wages, but contentment. To do as we like will only make us self-centred missiles, aimed at destroying our civilization, as happened with Rome and other civilizations. Why become Satan's pawns? We've found a lasting answer when we know how to submit ourselves to injustice, inequality and even hatred, without the inner reflexes of resentment, resistance and bitterness. These latter are what cause so much mental illness, far more than the former, and we older folk fear that young people today may head for a bigger harvest of trouble than we produced in our day.

Q. *Is there hope only for the Christian, then?*

A. It would not be right to say that, though the Christian should have the most on his side, having begun with submission. The trouble is that so many have submitted themselves, thus gaining inner peace in the midst of a grievous conflict, but have left the matter there. They have not gone on to tackle these things in the biblical way, as did Livingstone and a host of others, and have failed to change their environment, let alone the world. Jesus has some scathing words for such people. While they've found an answer for their own life, they've missed the great purpose that should flow from it, namely, changing the world about them by prayer and faith.

Q. *Should a Christian take part in strikes and such-like?*

A. Of course not. There is a better way. Paul tells the Christian to submit to his boss, as if he were submitting to Christ Himself (Eph. 6. 5). The Christian is instructed to work for his employer as though he were working alone for God and doing His will. This certainly eliminates boss-problems! Any difficulties may then be effectively committed to God in prayer and trust.

Q. *But that would make the Christian a hopeless sucker!*

A. On the contrary, it will give him a strength which in time will effectively topple the greed, unrighteousness and bludgeoning of any boss. Granted, it will mean that the Christian has no defence, but the God in whom he trusts will deliver him from that personality-destroyer called covetousness, and the other tensions that go with it. You should know how effective were the reforms produced by General Booth, for example. You are enjoying the benefits of some of those today. Yes, in the extreme case, the Christian is without a court of appeal, so that he may even have to die, simply because he will not fight back for himself; but before you object too violently, let me remind you that this was *the* way shown by Jesus Himself. Without any defence, and even rebuking Peter for drawing a sword on His behalf, He submitted to death by crucifixion. Tell me, did that change human history? and, if so, was it for better or for worse? The manifestation of the greatest love is not for a better deal for oneself, but to lay down one's life for his friend.

Q. *I concede your point about Jesus. But we——*

A. The same thing happened with Stephen. That brilliant life was as saturated with faith and the Holy Spirit as any man's in the New Testament. When the great moment arrived for a battle against injustice, he did not fight back, but submitted to death by stoning. Instead of cursing his murderers, he was free of bitterness on the inside to such an extent that he prayed God to forgive them! Who can neasure the triumph of that victory? It led straight to the conversion of the man who became the apostle Paul, greatest missionary to Europe. The same Paul, whose work still stands today, wrote to us to be "looking unto Jesus . . . Who . . . endured such contradiction of sinners against Himself, lest ye be wearied and faint in your minds. Ye have not yet resisted unto blood, striving against sin" (Heb. 12. 2–4).

Q. *Just a moment! Where are you taking me? Is martyrdom life's greatest purpose?*

A. Not necessarily, though it could be. Much will depend on where you fit into God's perfect plan to liberate a world fettered with sin, self and Satan. This is why the Christian has to choose between anarchism —which is the world's poor attempt at forcing liberty —and submission to the will of God, which *makes* people free! To be made free is far greater than to be set free. If you will accept it, the Bible plainly tells us what life's purpose is; but would you listen if I told you?

Q. *Do you mean to tell me that you know? Everybody is trying to find out what life is all about. Tell me, if you can!*

A. Now then! Why won't you read the Bible? I submit that if ever anyone found the purpose of life and fulfilled its purpose, it was Jesus Christ. History bears ample evidence of this, though that life ended at thirty-three years. No other person did so much for mankind. He gave the simple secret of His life as follows—to do the will of God and to finish His (the Father's) work (John 4. 34). In other words, He knew for what purpose He was here; He knew exactly what God desired Him to accomplish in word and work; He knew how to end His life. What is greater than these things?

Q. *But we cannot compare ourselves with the Son of God.*

A. How right you are! But we need to follow His example. What life could ever be fulfilled without the same two conditions? It can begin only when the life is submitted to Jesus Christ, first in salvation and then in discipleship. This was the secret of Stephen's life. Not longevity, but long effect! Though his life was cut short, it fulfilled God's will and he left behind him such a fantastic sermon that it has blessed millions of lives for nearly twenty centuries! Pretty effective, huh? But this was not God's plan for the life of Hudson Taylor, for example. Taylor sought and found God's will for his life as a young man, he went to China as a missionary and fulfilled God's mighty plan for himself and for China. Though he is long since dead, the work continues. Who can measure whose life was better?— James, who was beheaded in prison because it was the summit of God's plan for his life, or Peter, who was delivered out of the hands of the same King Herod by a miracle, because the works appointed for him were not yet complete? Let's get back to where we started: the very restlessness that young people feel within them is a divinely installed searching to come to know God, so that His will may be known for their lives, and what the outworking of that will is going to mean. To discover that will (and the road is open to all) is to live a full life and make an indelible mark on history for righteousness and for God. But to miss that will is to spell out the greatest possible human tragedy, and cause in this generation the same disillusionment as that of past generations who have missed life's purpose.

SUNDAY OBSERVANCE

Q. *I got a shock the other day. Last Sunday, as I was leaving church, I happened to mention to a friend that I was going to spend the afternoon playing football. Someone overheard me and gave me such a black look, mumbling something about not keeping the Sabbath. What did he mean?*

A. He probably meant that it is not good for you to spend your Sunday afternoon in such a manner now that you are a Christian.

Q. *Why not? I'm not harming anyone. What's wrong in exercising and keeping fit for the coming week? Doesn't the Bible command us to relax on Sundays?*

A. Your questions will have to be answered in stages. Let me tell you about the Sabbath first, and its difference from the Christian Sunday. In Genesis chapter two the Bible tells us that on the seventh day of creation God rested from all His labours. He then set apart every seventh day for man to do likewise, as it is the perfect pattern and a basic factor for good physical and mental health. The word "sabbath" means "cessation", for God ceased His work of creation. It was not until Moses received the Ten Commandments, however, that the Israelites were commanded to observe this day with extreme strictness. Failure to keep it met with the death penalty. In more recent times, some countries have tried other lengths of week, introducing a 6-day or an 8-day week, but have been compelled to give it up. The 7-day pattern is the only satisfactory one. We are made that way!

Q. *That old law was rough, wasn't it? Why don't we keep it now? Mind you, if we did, most of our people would have to face the death penalty!*

A. Let me finish answering your previous question along with the diversion! Remember that this Commandment was given solely to Israel, for it was with them that God made the covenant. In addition, the Sabbath became the sign of that covenant (Exod. 31. 13). This covenant had nothing to do with Gentile nations, for the simple reason that when two people make a covenant it is between them alone and not others. God never made the covenant of Ten Commandments with the Gentiles, for Israel were His special people, deliberately chosen from all the nations to keep His commandments and show forth His glory. Have you ever noticed that nearly all our calendars show Saturday as being the seventh day of the week?

Q. *It had never really occurred to me. Why don't we keep Saturday?*

A. Because the Church of God is under no obligation by divine law or covenant to do so.

Q. *What about the other Commandments, then? Does that make us free to steal, murder or bear false witness?*

A. No fear! The true believer, indwelt by the Holy Spirit, brings forth the fruit of the Spirit, which is love, joy, peace, long-suffering, gentleness, etc. When all nine of these (study Gal. 5. 22, 23) are manifested in the life, they lift us *above* the law. God gave the law for offenders, not for those who have been transformed through receiving a new heart. With love, joy and peace, could you murder someone, or steal? Similarly, instead of one day of rest in seven, the Christian enters a realm of rest which was established by the One who said, "Come unto Me, all ye that labour . . . and I will give you rest" (Matt. 11. 28).

Q. *Why all the fuss about Sunday, then?*

A. We set aside Sunday for three reasons: first, it is the day on which Jesus rose from the dead. It marks the day of a new finished work—the work of redemption through Jesus Christ. Secondly, although the New Testament does not command the keeping of either Sunday or Sabbath, we are given a good example of what the early church did in Acts 20. 7—"And upon the first day of the week, when the disciples came together to break bread (that is, the Holy Communion or the Lord's Supper), Paul preached unto them." That was the day on which they used to meet together. Thirdly, Christians generally like to set aside one day of the week to the Lord, and from what John said in Revelation 1. 10, we call it "the Lord's day". It is not altogether clear whether John was referring to the day of the week, or to the great coming "Day of the Lord", for he simply says, "I was in the Spirit on the Lord's day." Whatever he meant, this is where the title came from.

Q. *Let me get this straight—did you say that the New Testament gives no direct command that we are to keep either the Sabbath or Sunday?*

A. Correct. The New Testament puts us under no such command. Don't forget, though, that your health may begin to suffer, as well as your Christian life, if you do not set aside one day's rest in seven.

Q. *That's my point! Playing soccer is healthy enough. Why put me under something which is only tradition? That settles it, doesn't it?*

A. No, not yet! If, for the Christian, Sunday is "the Lord's day", and you are the Lord's servant, will you begin to make it your *own* day? His love has given us much liberty, yet that love looks for a willing response. Instead of liberty to do what pleases us, this liberty is so great that it enables us to do what pleases Him. In Romans 14. 5 we read, "One man esteemeth one day above another: another esteemeth every day alike. Let every man be fully persuaded in his own mind." This liberty is to be used, not abused. Most people only work a five-day week now, which gives you one whole day for your soccer. Can you not give Sunday wholly to the Lord? I think it is best for a Christian to live *every* day fully to the Lord, with Sunday as the crowning blessing! When we stop to think what it cost God to provide for our salvation, surely the least we can do is to set aside Sunday solely for Him, in worship and service, doing His will, instead of indulging ourselves.

Q. *Yes, that's reasonable enough. Are there any more verses like Romans 14. 5?*

A. Listen to this one in Colossians 2. 16. "Allow no one therefore to take you to task about what you eat or drink, or over the observance of festival, new moon, or sabbath." We are not to be in bondage to any of these things and therefore cannot be condemned for not obeying the details of the old law, which had much to say about what should and should not be eaten, about the Passover and the Sabbath.

Q. *That verse strengthens my case powerfully, doesn't it?*

A. Legally, yes. Don't brush aside what we have already said, of course. There is a big matter to consider with this verse—that we should put ourselves in the position where people will not judge us. Romans 14. 15, 16 tells us to be careful not to stumble those who are weak in the faith, even when we are in the right. You see, for centuries, in Britain, Sunday observance has been interpreted as meaning, among other things, that a Christian does not indulge himself in Sunday soccer. If you ride rough-shod over this you will only prove to be a stumbling-block to others, who will wonder what kind of a Christian you are. Keep out of the position, says the verse, where others can take you to task about your behaviour. But there's another point—you have six days in which to earn your living, with plenty of time for recreation. Is it asking too much, if you are not going to serve God full-time, to set aside one day in which to do His will?

Q. *Stop! That convinces me. But just one more question. What do I do about working overtime on Sundays?*

A. The New Testament is silent, and therefore I can only give you my counsel as a servant of the Lord. First, don't shirk your load of work. Many become ineffective witnesses for Christ in that way. Never use your Christianity as an excuse to avoid an unpleasant duty. Be always ready to deny yourself. Secondly, ask for permission to work your overtime on a weekday, if possible. The overtime rate is less then, but, if you do it for the Lord's sake, your sincerity will be noticed and this will validate your words among those with whom you work. Thirdly, failing all else, go to work and commit your cause to God in prayer and faith.

EVANGELISTIC GIMMICKS

Q. *Should Christians copy "the world" in their attempt to win them to Christ?*

A. A lot depends in which way they want to copy them. The late General Booth of the Salvation Army introduced Christian songs put to popular music in a bid to reach ordinary people. The popular music of those days did not have some of the destructive elements which some music has today, and therefore there was little danger of harm being done. I must say, as an ex-jazz musician, that I have never expected to hear, nor have been attracted by the use of jazz music in evangelistic rallies or church services, and have always found it difficult to know why Christians lean so much in this direction. In fact, a friend of mine who played in one of the most successful Christian musical teams of the last decade in Britain told me that, while their music attracted many thousands of listeners, the number converted was tragically small by comparison.

Q. *Maybe, but even if one was saved is that not sufficient justification for it?*

A. Most decidedly, if you look at it from that sole point of view. But is there not a better way of doing the job? I mean, it takes a lot of work, practice and considerable expense to produce a worthwhile team, and, even when this is done, is it our business to attract outsiders in this way? If our music is "as good as theirs", we usually project ourselves to the exclusion of our Saviour and make it difficult for them to receive

F

our message. Let us win people to Christ by every possible means, yet it seems to me that we should be honest enough to assess the result and discard what is not sufficiently profitable to justify its continuance.

Q. *Granted, but did not Paul say something about being all things to all men?*

A. Yes, he did, but we should not ignore the context in which he said it. You see, how are you going to reach adulterers? Would you do it by opening a "Christian brothel"? A thousand times no! How are you going to reach thieves and murderers by this approach? We are talking about extremes, I know, but the same principle applies to lesser things. When I used to be involved in Sunday school work we soon discovered that using 'bait' to get the kids to come did more harm than good in the long run, and we had to drop it before it broke up the work.

Q. *It's all right to criticize, but what would you do instead? It's tough getting folk into Christian meetings these days.*

A. Is it? I thought the reverse was true. I suppose a lot depends on where you get your information. Some places are suffering a backlash, true, from having used gimmicks too much in the past, and now have either closed their work or made radical changes to it. What is wrong with the age-tested method of prevailing prayer and the power of God, both in preaching and in demonstration of God's power through the evidence of His working?

Q. *Before we get to that, what do you think about something like "Jesus Christ Superstar"?*

A. We have switched from your original enquiry

about evangelism, but rather than discuss the text of that performance, on which there have been so many differing views, I think there is an overriding principle involved with things of that kind which Paul spoke of when he wrote to the Christians at Philippi: "Some indeed preach Christ from envy and rivalry, but others from good will. The latter do it out of love, knowing that I am put here for the defence of the gospel; the former proclaim Christ out of partisanship, not sincerely but thinking to afflict me in my imprisonment. What then? Only that in every way, whether in pretence or in truth, Christ is proclaimed; and in that I rejoice" (Phil. 1. 15–18).

Q. *That's quite a point! Would you say the same about pop records of Jesus?*

A. Yes, I would. For my part I fail to see how the noise and hardly audible words one so often hears can do any good for the gospel, but it thrills me when I go into a shop and see a record sleeve among the discs with the name "Jesus" on it. It is marvellous that His name is appearing in all sorts of places, and I am confident that the Holy Spirit knows how to do His own job, for there is a mighty power in that name. Mind you, a 'popular' Christ is not going to do much for people eternally, but the genuine seekers will leave all that behind and seek the true Christ.

Q. *What about taking Christ into the world of entertainment?*

A. I am all for taking Him into every possible place. Wherever you can find sinners, they need Jesus. But here again I think those involved in this kind of thing should be careful to see that what they *do* does not negate what they *say*. They need to be desperately honest about their motives and their results, to see whether a genuine work for God is being accomplished. If the spiritual quality is poor and the results small, I would think it wiser to be rid of the method and get down to a more profitable basis of presentation, for on the Great Day we are going to be judged on what we have done in the flesh. The man who produced ten pounds in the parable had double the reward of the man who only produced five. I don't think this is mercenary, if what we do is done for His glory, but it is God Himself who asks us to consider what we are doing in relation to the Great Day.

Q. *What about Christian acting?*

A. Why act when you can be real? Again, while it is good to use anything which will reach people for Christ, we must remember that God has not chosen acting, but He has chosen preaching as the most effective way of getting the job of evangelism done. Preaching is a foolish method really, but this is why God chose it, so that the hindrance of "impressing people by our ability" may be minimized. As it is, we still try to impress people by techniques of preaching, sorry to say! However, on the subject of plays and acting, I sympathize with the BBC and similar institutions for having to choose their plays from the productions of men and women who betray an obsession with sex, vulgarity and so on. I believe Christians should counteract this by those gifted in this realm getting down to the playwriting business themselves, supplying the media with a better quality product morally and in every other way. Christians should accept this challenge sanely and responsibly, instead of hurling constant criticism. But that is a different thing to your question about evangelism.

Q. *No matter. And what about Christian-Hippy communes?*

A. It seems to me that there is nothing more ideal for Hippies, once they are converted, than bringing them into Christian communes. I would go so far as to say there is a necessity for this. But those involved in this work should not begin to say that this type of living is the only scriptural way for all Christians. Communes were available for the early Jewish Christians in Palestine because they were cut off by their families as soon as they were converted and had no other way to subsist. It was an emergency measure, but not a pattern to be adopted by Christians universally. The gentile Christians did not live in communes, as seen when Paul wrote thus to the Corinthians: "Can't you do your eating and drinking at home?" (1 Cor. 11. 22.) We are also told that they had communion services and Bible studies from house to house. I would recommend to those working with saved Hippies that they should try to prepare them to take their place in a responsible church community.

Q. *Is there a Bible precedent for not using good modern techniques in evangelism?*

A. As it is a book which relates what happened through the power of God, there is little written about techniques to draw from, but I suppose we could take an example from what happened when King David decided to bring the Ark of the Covenant up to Jerusalem and put it in a special and central place. He called his chiefs of staff and the nation's leaders together and outlined his plan to bring the ark to Jerusalem on a newly constructed cart, accompanied by a great procession and much royal pomp. The plan was warmly endorsed by unanimous vote. The cart was constructed and an unfortunate man from the tribe of Judah chosen, Uzzah by name, to supervise its journey and care. All went well until the oxen drawing the cart stumbled and the ark began to slip from the cart. Uzzah stretched out his hand and steadied it, the obvious thing to do, but then tragedy struck without warning or precedent: God smote him and he died on the spot. That wrecked the procession and people went home shocked, not least of all David himself.

Q. *Where did he get the idea of the cart from?*

A. The Philistines! The ark had been missing from its proper place ever since the Israelites had taken it to war as a victory mascot, and lost it. But when the Philistines captured it they discovered that the God of this ark began to plague them with violent sicknesses, so much so that they sent it back with a penance gift of gold symbols. They built a new cart to carry it and hitched it to a span of cows that had just calved and had never been yoked, and sent it back on its own. Miraculously the span took that ark straight over to the Israelites and after an unfortunate incident at Beth-shemesh, involving the death of certain men who opened it inquisitively, it was deposited in the home of Abinadab, where it remained for twenty years until David fetched it (1 Sam. chap. 6 and 7). Could it have been that the whole miraculous incident impressed David in an unfortunate way?

Q. *Did he ever discover the right way to handle it, for he finally brought it to Jerusalem?*

A. Oh, yes. David went straight home after the Uzzah tragedy and searched the Scriptures until he found out that the only people permitted to handle the ark were Levites. With this knowledge he started again, having been encouraged by hearing that the home of the man where they had left the ark following the accident had been unusually blessed. The Levites were appointed for the job, and, after suitable sacrifices had been offered, the ark was brought up without incident, but with great triumph, to Jerusalem.

Q. *Sorry, but what is the application in all of this? I must be a bit thick.*
A. The application is that if the 'ark' (symbolizing the presence of Christ) is to be brought into our city, or factory, or area, it must be accomplished by people whom God has anointed to do it. Not only that, but evangelism should be done in God's way; and by that I do not mean it should follow some stereotyped pattern that might have been useful for the last generation.

Q. *How do you find anointed people and the divine pattern?*
A. Those who are concerned about evangelizing their town, or factory, or what-have-you, need to seek God earnestly in prayer until He reveals what He wants done and how He wishes it to be carried out. To conduct an evangelistic effort just because of an idea, or an obvious need, is insufficient reason. Too often there is a tendency to adopt a 'standard' method or to think out some new approach and then ask God to bless it. It is better to wait upon God and seek His counsel until He reveals what is to be done, and how, and by whom. Then God will supply the power to do it. He is only obliged to see through what He has initiated. This *is* the way of maximum fruitfulness, and producing fruit which will continue. The way to know that God is in it is to wait until He puts an 'amen' in your heart: that is, His 'Yes' and the knowledge of His

mind. Thereafter, faith is neither tempting God nor hoping for the best, but obedience to what He has revealed, against whatever odds.

Q. *What place do our natural talents have in all of this?*

A. The inherent problem with talents in Christian work is that they often magnify the performers and draw the praise in their direction. The Holy Spirit draws men to Christ, not by admiring His followers, but by convincing them of sin, righteousness and judgment. He wants worshippers, not hero-worshippers. Unless talented people are anointed by God's Spirit, they are not only impotent to do a proper spiritual work, but can do more harm than good. But there is one more thing: people are in great need everywhere, and the early church ministered Christ to the people at every level, healing the sick and those who were oppressed. We should not be put off by any pseudo attempts which we might have heard of in the recent past. We only need to see His delivering power ministered at every level in effectiveness, such as when the apostles healed the man at the Gate Beautiful, in Acts chapter three, and the need for advertising and gimmicks will become unnecessary, or at least minimal, and even ludicrous. The standard is high, but let us press on to attain it.

CHRISTIAN UNITY

Q. *I am thrilled with the prospect of there being only one Church soon, aren't you?*

A. Why do you say "soon"? Ever since the Lord Jesus constituted His Church it has always and only been one.

Q. *Awww—come off it! Aren't you refusing to face up to clear facts? You know that we are split from head to foot with denominations.*

A. No, I don't think I'm refusing to face facts. You need to see the whole thing from God's point of view. I agree at once that we are overloaded with man-made, man-organized, man-controlled and man-sustained churches, but have you never read what the Lord Jesus Himself said—"*I* will build My Church; and the gates of hell shall not prevail against it"? (Matt. 16. 18.) If you look back over history you will readily see that Christians have always tried to organize movements of God into a human framework. Whenever the Holy Spirit has restored to the Church important truths which have been either lost or neglected, men have soon elevated them out of proportion and isolated them behind denominational walls, instead of continuing to be led on by the Holy Spirit. Ever since the Fall man has vied with God for control. In the same way that it is God alone who can save a soul, so it is only the Lord who can build the true Church, and He said so! In building it He may use whom He will; but the prerogative is His, not theirs. He is essentially Head of the Church and shares this headship with none.

Q. *Don't you believe it would be better, therefore, just for that reason, to be united into a great world church? That would accomplish what you are advocating.*

A. The heart of every true believer should long to be united with every other believer, but that unity must stand on a right foundation. John said, "Our fellowship is with the Father, and with His Son Jesus Christ" (1 John 1. 3). *He* is the basis for our unity, not a carefully adjusted compromise which suits denominational leaders or followers, while not agreeing with the truth.

Q. *Ah—snag! Who is going to set the standard of truth?*

A. I don't think you are wise to approach the matter in that way. This was the way that brought Pilate to grief, for when Jesus said to him, "Every one that is of the truth heareth My voice", he retorted with a cynical "What is truth?" Then he never waited for the reply to his own enquiry and he thereby shut the door to any further revelation entering his heart.

Q. *I'm sorry! What, then, is the truth regarding this matter?*

A. Jesus told His disciples, "Howbeit when He, the Spirit of truth, is come, *He* will guide you into all truth" (John 16. 13). He alone is the One to set the standard, but the flesh finds it mighty hard to be led by the Spirit, because His leading necessitates a crucifying of self and self-domination. If you look around the religious world today you will see that two main things are happening on the Christian front: on one side men are meeting around conference tables and bartering the truth with each other so as to reach a place of agreement. Here we see a desperate struggle by self not to lose its control. The main consideration is not the glorious standard set by the Word of God, but a standard low enough to be acceptable to their various interpretations of it. The possibility of unity appeals to us all, because deep down we know that Christians should be united. However, truths for which our fathers in the faith have shed their blood are being glossed over in the big bid for unity. But on the other side we see God fulfilling His promise to the prophet Joel to pour out His Spirit upon all flesh. This is affecting believers of most denominations and is binding them together into a unity that is based upon Himself.

Q. *Does that mean we should all quit our churches and get out?*

A. Assuredly not. That would result in yet another denomination being formed, and we should be back where we started. You seem to find it hard to grasp that the Church is not a man-organized affair, but His Body. Jesus said that He is the Vine, and we are the branches. Consider, now, that the Vine is the whole plant, branches and all. For the most explicit definition of the Church, it is Jesus Christ—in His people. But while leaving our churches may be pointless, the time may well come, if this man-made unity succeeds, when those who refuse to compromise certain fundamental truths concerning the faith may be expelled from their churches, but that is quite a different matter and not one which should be either anticipated or precipitated by the wholehearted follower of the Lord Jesus. Our allegiance, within our denomination, must be first and foremost to the Lord. On the Great Day we shall give account to *Him* for our obedience (or otherwise) to the truth, and therefore we should live now with that day in view.

Q. *Hmmm! Won't that produce a lot of fifth colum-nists in our denominations? Would it not be better if they DID get out?*

A. There will be no fifth column if we follow Paul's definition of a Spirit-filled Christian in Ephesians 5. 18–21, where he says that such should submit them-selves to one another in the fear of the Lord. God would never ask a Spirit-filled person to submit them-selves to untruth, but they can submit themselves to a *person* who does not hold the truth. This is exactly what the Master did, even though that path of love took Him to the cross. In this present-day outpouring of the Spirit it is gratifying to see that those being filled with the Holy Spirit are not, in the main, hiving off to other churches, but, rather, bearing witness right where they are. It is also encouraging to see that few are being expelled, and while this continues there is hope of a wider spread of blessing. I would remind you that the Church, as God sees it, is not a man-made organization, but a God-breathed organism. God sees it as a body, not a machine, and the head of this body is the Lord Jesus Himself and not anyone to whom He may have entrusted a ministry for the building up of that body. It is a pity that so many think of the head being far away in heaven and the body down here on the earth. Any body in such a situation would be life-less, and perhaps this accounts for the deadness of many churches.

Q. *Why did God allow the Church to get so out of hand?*

A. Out of whose hand? The Church which He is building is not out of hand, but right *in* His mighty hand! Jesus foreshadowed what would happen, though, in His parable of the wheat and the tares. In the parable He declared Himself to be the sower of the true seed. But the enemy, Satan, sowed false seed in the same field. When it was discovered that tares were springing up along with the wheat, the servants wanted to uproot them at once. But He gave instructions that they should be left to grow together until the harvest by the angels at the end of the age. Never forget that, because of the great underlying principle of divine love. God has given to man a free will. When we become Christians that free will remains, but should be immediately submitted to His authority. If we choose to disobey the truth, we may do so, and pay the price of disobedience later. Denominational trouble hit the church at Corinth, for example; and, though not affecting their doctrines, it did affect the persons. Paul remonstrated with them, saying, "For while one saith, I am of Paul; and another, I am of Apollos; are ye not carnal?" (1 Cor. 3. 4.) This division between the believers marked their carnality and desire for human leadership. Whatever truth the Spirit reveals to us gives us no ground for separating ourselves from any other who has been cleansed by the precious blood of Christ and born again of His Holy Spirit.

Q. *I get it now! In our churches we should be loyal to each other, not building up a denominational spirit, but building up the body of Christ. Right?*

A. Right! And remember that the final test of divine love is a willingness to lay our lives down, if necessary, so as to bring life and truth to those who do not possess them. Many are coveting the Spirit's gifts for their own gratification, but that is only an evidence of selfish Christianity. 1 Corinthians 12. 31 urges us to seek these same gifts by a better way than coveting, namely, with love. In other words, those in need must be in the centre of our focus when seeking, and that is why 1 Corinthians 13 was written.

To sum up, let us recognize Christ's headship in the Church and build what He is building. If we choose to build that which man is building outside of His will, then let us not be surprised to see it go on the final bonfire, while we stand before Him with empty hands.